FAMILY CELEBRATIONS AT EASTER

FAMILY CELEBRATIONS AT EASTER

Ann Hibbard

A Raven's Ridge Book

Baker Books

A Division of Baker Book House Co
Grand Rapids, Michigan 49516

Scripture quotations, unless otherwise marked are taken from the New International Version (NIV), copyright © 1973, 1978, 1984, International Bible Society. Used by permission of Zondervan Bible Publishers.

Hymns, unless otherwise noted are in the public domain and no copyright acknowledgement is necessary. *All Glory, Laud, and Honor* from *Neues Choralbuch* © 1970 Baerenreiter Music Corporation, is used by permission of Baerenreiter Music Corporation. *Jesus, Priceless Treasure*, from *Orgelchoralbuch Württemberg* © Gesangbuch-verlag der Evangelischen Landeskirche Württemburg, Stgt. Used by permission.

ISBN: 0-8010-4390-5

Second printing, March 1994

Printed in the United States of America

Contents

A FRESH APPROACH
TO EASTER

It was one of those Kodak moments. Our two pajama-clad preschoolers scoured the living room and dining room pouncing on tiny football-shaped chocolate eggs wrapped in bright foil. Each had a basket slung over an arm as they raced madly from one hiding spot to the next. I was just as excited as they were, shouting hints and exclaiming over their discoveries. Yet deep within me, I harbored a gnawing sense that something was missing.

Later that morning we dropped the kids off at the church nursery and we settled in to our seats in the sanctuary. Trumpet-like white lilies decorated the altar, and their sweet fragrance filled the air. As we sang the stirring refrains of "Jesus Christ Is Risen Today! Alleluia!" I again felt a tug at my heart.

This is what Easter is all about, I thought. But do my children know that? Can I somehow get them as excited about Jesus as they are about Easter baskets?

Easter egg hunts and chocolate candies inspire great enthusiasm in children! But how can we as Christian parents inspire in our children appreciation for Jesus' death and excitement for his resurrection?

It is the Christmas dilemma all over again, except that Christmas is easier in some respects. Children readily grasp the idea of a sweet little baby in a manger. Stars, angels, and sheep on a hillside form lovely pictures in a child's mind.

Easter is a bit trickier, however. The cross is not a comfortable image. Suffering and death are subjects that most adults want to avoid, and they certainly don't relish tackling them with their young children. Easter is a bit easier than Good Friday; Easter at least is a happy celebration. But the resurrection is difficult for many adults to understand. It raises its own set of thorny questions.

Let's face it, the Easter bunny is the safest route to take! If we talk about springtime and new life, we won't have to deal with the nasty business of the crucifixion. Leave those hard truths for later, when our children are older and better able to handle them, some insist.

Unfortunately, when "later" comes, chances are those children will be listening to the voices of friends and teachers more than the voices of their parents. It is during the early and pre-adolescent years that a child's heart is fertile for the planting of the parents' faith and values.

If we neglect to teach our children about Jesus' death and resurrection, we miss a wonderful, natural opportunity to lead our children to faith in Jesus Christ.

But most of us do not feel up to such a daunting task. How can we explain these things to our children? We enjoy seeing our children excited and happy at Easter. Yet a gnawing restlessness reminds us that we aren't giving our kids the full picture.

Won't talk of death and resurrection put a damper on their enthusiasm? Is it possible to evoke that level of enthusiasm in our children for matters of faith?

The answer is yes! Here's how:

Shoot Straight

Do not be afraid to shoot straight with your children about spiritual things. I find that adults underestimate children's ability to grasp and accept spiritual truths.

One of my earliest memories is of a picture of the crucifixion. My grandmother had a King James Bible at her home which had about a dozen color illustrations interspersed throughout the pages. As a child of two or three, I was fascinated by these pictures, particularly the one of Jesus hanging on the cross. "Poor Jesus!" I murmured mournfully.

Even at that tender age, my heart was responsive to Christ. I may not have understood the theology of the substitutionary death of Christ, but I knew that I loved "poor Jesus!"

Children have an uncanny ability to absorb the things that they can process and to dismiss the things that they cannot.

We want so much to shield our children from pain. The fact is, however, that life is full of suffering. And no matter how hard we try to protect our children, they will encounter pain.

Rather than avoiding the subject of pain, we need to show our children where they can find comfort when they are in pain. What better place than in the arms of "poor Jesus," the one who knows suffering?

Several years ago, our much-loved puppy Josie was hit by a car and killed. The pain in our hearts seemed more than we could bear. In the midst of our grief, we found comfort in knowing that Jesus understood our sorrow. Together we read Isaiah 53 where Jesus is described as "a man of sorrows, and familiar with suffering." The deep ache of grief remained, but knowing that Jesus cared and could feel our hurt somehow brought us comfort and peace.

Small children may not fully comprehend what it means that Jesus died on the cross to save them from their sin. But they know what it feels like to hurt. If they can learn that Jesus was hurt very badly, then they can bring their hurts to Jesus and find comfort

Now that our children are entering their teens, they encounter new kinds of hurts. Both have suffered ridicule and rejection from peers. How I hurt for them during those times! Yet it comforts us to remember that Jesus too faced ridicule and rejection. He too was abandoned by his friends.

The message of the cross is the message of salvation, yes, but of comfort as well. And in a world of pain, it is a message that our children need to hear.

Speak on Their Terms

To be effective with our children, we need to speak on their level. Big words and long prayers just won't do it!

Most of us are so immersed in our adult concerns that we forget what life looks like from a child's point of view.

Asking simple questions of our children can unlock the door to their thoughts, fears, questions, and dreams. For example, ask your child, "What do you think about as you are falling asleep?" As she answers, remind yourself not to correct any of her "wrong" notions. Your purpose is to get to know what she is thinking and feeling. Only when we begin to understand our children can we effectively communicate our faith with them.

Life provides many "teachable moments," when a conversation or situation is a natural lead-in for communicating spiritual truth. Springtime is a wonderful time to teach our children about resurrection. They love to get their hands dirty in the garden, working beside Mom or Dad. Jesus himself told the story of the seed dying in order to bring forth life. We can use this moment to talk about how Jesus had to die so that he could give us new life. Just like the new green shoot coming out of the earth, Jesus came out of the grave with a new body.

Children learn best when they are able to employ as many senses as possible. Our church has a fantastic Good Friday service for small children. The children are taken in groups to various stations where they learn about one aspect of Jesus' death or resurrection. At each station there is something physical for the children to eat, drink, smell, see, or touch. I manned the "crown of thorns" station. I had fashioned a real crown of thorns out of rose stems. I asked the children to touch a thorn and feel how sharp it was. Then the children were each given a miniature crown of thorns made from brown pipe cleaners. Such hands-on experiences make a vivid impression on children and help them to understand the Easter story.

Seek God

Finally, if we want our children to become excited about Jesus, that same excitement must be evident in our lives. We cannot fake it. Children are not fooled. They know the genuine article.

I have a vivid recollection of one particular Good Friday of my childhood. Mom gathered us around her and opened a slim gray volume, the gospel of Luke, paraphrased by J. B. Phillips.

"Today we remember what Jesus did for us by dying on the cross," she began. "I'd like for us to read the story of the crucifixion."

Mom is not a dramatic reader, yet I found myself spell-bound. The story itself was gripping. Luke's account, retold in language that I could understand, transported me to the garden of Gethsemane, Pilate's courtyard, the hill of Golgotha. I felt as though I were there. Even though I had heard these verses from early childhood, this time I heard them anew.

For Mom, there was nothing more important in all of life than faith in Jesus Christ. Her faith was genuine. As I grew up, I made that faith my own.

I know of no better way to grow in a genuine faith than to spend time with the Lord, in worship, in prayer, and in regular Bible reading and study. Ask God to give you understanding. He has promised that if we earnestly seek him, we will find him. He wants to reveal his truth to us.

A heart that is open to God will soon be filled with a joy that spills over into the lives around it. Your children will see the difference in you, just as I saw the difference my mother's faith made in her life. Genuine faith is the only kind of faith that is infectious.

Then, seek God together, as a family. I don't recommend that you wait until Good Friday. Begin at Ash Wednesday, six and a half weeks before Easter. Take ten minutes a day, either every day, or at least once a week, to read a few Bible verses from an easy-to-understand translation. Follow this up with two or three age-appropriate questions and a brief prayer. Older children and especially musical families will enjoy singing together some of the wonderful hymns of the season.

Family times like these have transformed our celebration of Easter.

Ten years have passed since that frenetic Easter egg hunt in the living room. My gnawing sense of "something missing" prompted me to find creative ways to make the Easter story real and exciting for my children. The initial awkwardness of explaining Christ's suffering gave way to tender moments of comfort. And that was only one facet of the Easter message. As we explored together, we uncovered a wealth of Easter gems with far-reaching significance for each of our lives.

Sure, we still get excited about chocolate Easter eggs. But better yet, I have learned how to inspire in my children excitement for the deeper truths of Easter. And that's real cause for celebration!

You are about to embark on a journey. You and your family are on your way to a new understanding and experience of Easter. *Family Celebrations at Easter* will guide you and your family along this thrilling path.

The focus of the book is the celebration of Lent, the traditional time of preparation for Easter. This six-and-one-half-week period provides families the opportunity to investigate Jesus' death and resurrection and what that means for us. *Family Celebrations at Easter* gives your family a full six and a half weeks of simple, child-oriented family devotions for this season of anticipation.

My favorite celebration of this season is Passover! This book includes a Messianic *Haggadah*, an order of service for a Christian celebration of Passover. Plenty of explanations and instructions are given—even a recipe for matzoh ball soup!

Finally, Easter itself: a short but meaningful family worship service is outlined, complete with words and music to favorite Easter hymns. And the "Holy Treasure Hunt" will have everyone hopping up and down in glee.

My prayer is that this Easter season will be your best ever family celebration!

A NOTE TO PARENTS

Perhaps you have wondered, as I did, how to make the message of Easter real to your children. The process began for me one year with a brainstorm. The kids love to hunt for hidden treasure. Why not find treasures that pertain to the events of Jesus' death and resurrection? That was the origin of our "Holy Treasure Hunt," page 116. The kids had a ball, and as we gathered together the treasures that they found, we talked about their meaning. I knew that they were learning about Jesus, but they thought that they were just having fun!

Then one December, as our family gathered for our Advent devotions, I thought, "We need to do this at Easter time! Preparing our hearts to celebrate Jesus' death and resurrection is even more important than preparing to celebrate his birth. More than anything else, I want my kids to understand why Jesus died and rose again—and what it means for us."

To that end, I have written Lenten Devotions. Since the early days of the church, Lent has been a season of self-examination, sorrow for sin, and commitment to Christ. It is the six-and-one-half-week period preceding Easter. These brief devotionals take your family inside the drama of Jesus' last days, his arrest, the crucifixion, and resurrection.

Carve out of your schedule just ten or fifteen minutes each evening after supper. As you read, discuss, and pray together, you will meet Christ as a family in a new way, and your Easter season will be rich with his presence.

Are you looking for an alternative to coloring Easter eggs? Make a Holiday Tree! This is a simple, hands-on project for the entire family. It is inexpensive and easy to make, and even toddlers can get involved. Best of all, it adds excitement and fun to the family devotional time as each evening the children get to hang one symbol on the Holiday Tree. Each symbol corresponds to the Scripture for that day, so the message is reinforced visually. (Instructions for making a Holiday Tree may be found on p. 152.)

Or your family may prefer to create a "Treasure Table." Designate a table in your family room or living area for this purpose—even a card table or coffee table will do. You may want to cover it with a tablecloth and set it in a corner. This is where you will place one item each day which corresponds to that day's devotional. Most items are simple household items (e.g., a sponge) or pictures cut out from magazines. Nothing could be simpler, yet it is a wonderful way to reinforce the Bible reading in the minds of children. Then, on Easter, you are all set for your Holy Treasure Hunt. The items are all collected—all you have to do is hide them (see p.116).

Each devotional includes:

Explain—A real-life story introduces the theme or the passage.

Read—The central theme or question for each devotional is emphasized in a passage from the New International Version of the Bible.

Discuss—There are several questions for younger children and several for older children and adults. These are meant to encourage understanding and discussion.

Final Thought—This is a brief summary of truths or insights drawn from the passage.

Pray—These prayers are short and to the point. Don't feel limited to the suggested prayer. Encourage your children to pray extemporaneously as well.

Sing—Words to one or two verses of a Lent or Easter hymn appear in the devotional itself. The entire hymn, words and music, may be found at the rear of this book on pages 180–196.

Do—This section instructs you as to which symbol to find and to hang on your Easter Tree.

Further Study for Adults—These are questions or suggestions for teens or adults who want to focus on these passages for their own personal quiet time or devotional time during Lent. Use a spiral notebook or steno pad as your Lenten journal. And get ready to grow!

Remember, do only those things which work with the ages and attention spans of your children. Feel free to change and adapt these ideas to suit the needs of your family.

FAMILY
CELEBRATIONS
AT
EASTER

LENTEN DEVOTIONS

Have you ever been in a club where only certain people were allowed in? What did people have to do to join? When my daughter Laura was in third grade, it seemed that clubs were the big thing with the girls in her class. The most popular girl was always the president of the club, and she chose who would belong and who wouldn't. Often Laura came home in tears because she was not allowed in the club. It is an awful feeling to be left out of the fun or excluded from a group.

As Jesus was traveling toward Jerusalem to suffer and die for us, he taught the people about the kingdom of God. Some people thought that the kingdom of God was like a club. They wanted to make sure that only the right people are allowed to join.

Read—*Luke 13:22–30*

Then Jesus went through the towns and villages, teaching as he made his way to Jerusalem. Someone asked him, "Lord, are only a few people going to be saved?"

He said to them, "Make every effort to enter through the narrow door, because many, I tell you, will try to enter and will not be able to. Once the owner of the house gets up and closes the door, you will stand outside knocking and pleading, 'Sir, open the door for us.'

"But he will answer, 'I don't know you or where you come from.'

"Then you will say, 'We ate and drank with you, and you taught in our streets.'

"But he will reply, 'I don't know you or where you come from. Away from me, all you evildoers!'

"There will be weeping there, and gnashing of teeth, when you see Abraham, Isaac and Jacob and all the prophets in the kingdom of God, but you yourselves thrown out. People will come from east and west and north and south, and will take their places at the feast in the kingdom of God. Indeed there are those who are last who will be first, and first who will be last."

Discuss

1. What question did someone ask Jesus?
2. Jesus answered by telling a story. Tell the story in your own words.
3. What did Jesus mean when he said that "there are those who are last who will be first, and first who will be last"?
4. How did Jesus' words make the people feel? Why?

Final Thought

Jesus' answer was not what these people wanted to hear. Jesus said, in effect, "Not everyone will be in the kingdom of God, but get ready for some surprises. People will be there that you don't expect. And some whom you were sure would be there, won't be. Make sure that you know you will be allowed in."

Jesus himself is "the narrow door." It is only by trusting in Jesus that we may enter God's kingdom or family. Are you in his family?

Pray

Dear Lord, thank you for coming to save us. Help me to tell my friends about you so that they too can be in your family.

Sing—*Just as I Am*

Just as I am, without one plea,
But that thy Blood was shed for me,
And that thou bidd'st me come to thee,
O Lamb of God, I come, I come.

Do

Place the symbol of the door on your holiday tree.

Further Study for Adults

Read Isaiah 50:6–7, a prophesy concerning the suffering of the Messiah. These words are echoed in Luke 9:51, where we read that Jesus "resolutely set out for Jerusalem." What do these two passages show us about the person of Jesus Christ?

When our family takes a trip, we pack up our car and get on an interstate highway. All the cars and trucks are barreling along at 65 miles per hour, and with the car windows down, conversation is impossible. Sometimes we take an airplane when we travel. A thousand miles fly by in a few short hours. We talk or read, eat a snack, and suddenly, we're landing! On a recent business trip, my plane flew through an electrical storm. Lightning was right outside our windows. That was a little too exciting for me!

What do you do to pass the time as you travel? One time-honored way to pass the time on a journey is to tell stories.

When Jesus took his last trip on earth, his trip to Jerusalem, he walked many miles on hot, dusty roads. And as he walked, he talked to people, answering questions, teaching, and telling stories. Here is one of the stories that Jesus told on that trip.

Read—*Luke 14:16–23*

Jesus replied: "A certain man was preparing a great banquet and invited many guests. At the time of the banquet he sent his servant to tell those who had been invited, 'Come, for everything is now ready.'

"But they all alike began to make excuses. The first said, 'I have just bought a field, and I must go and see it. Please excuse me.'

"Another said, 'I have just bought five yoke of oxen, and I'm on my way to try them out. Please excuse me.'

"Still another said, 'I just got married, so I can't come.'

"The servant came back and reported this to his master. Then the owner of the house became angry and ordered his servant, 'Go out quickly into the streets and alleys of the town and bring in the poor, the crippled, the blind and the lame.'

"'Sir,' the servant said, 'what you ordered has been done, but there is still room.'

"Then the master told his servant, 'Go out to the roads and country lanes and make them come in, so that my house will be full.'"

Discuss

1. Pretend that you were having the most fantastic birthday party ever—but everyone you invited said they couldn't come. How would you feel?
2. What did the man giving the party in Jesus' story do?
3. A parable is a story with a meaning. In this parable, the man giving the party is God. Whom did the first guests represent? The second group of guests? What message was Jesus giving the Jews through this story?
4. When God calls us to know him or spend time with him, sometimes we have excuses, too. What are some of the excuses we use instead of accepting God's invitations?

Final Thought

God is always calling us to know him better. Psalm 34:8 says "Taste and see that the Lord is good." Knowing God is like enjoying a wonderful feast. And we are invited because of what Jesus did on the cross for us. Those who accept will have a seat at God's glorious banquet in heaven.

Pray

Dear Lord, thank you for inviting me to the feast. Help me not to make excuses, but simply to accept your invitation.

Sing—*Just as I Am*

Just as I am, poor, wretched, blind;
Sight, riches, healing of the mind,
Yea, all I need, in thee to find,
O Lamb of God, I come, I come.

Do

Place the symbol of the roast turkey on your holiday tree.

Further Study for Adults

Read Isaiah 25:6–9 and Revelation 19:9. What do we learn about the heavenly banquet from these passages?

FRIDAY

WEEK ONE

Have you ever known anyone who thought he was perfect and everyone else was not nearly as good as he was? Perhaps the person you are thinking of likes to brag and boast. Have you ever felt or acted that way? I must confess that I am a terrible boaster. I love to show off. When I've worked hard on something, like sewing curtains for our home, I like to show off what I have done. It feels good to hear people say nice things about my work. Or when I have gotten a good deal on something, such as finding a beautiful silk dress at a thrift shop for eight dollars, I can't resist telling people. That makes me look smart and economical.

What things do you boast about? We all want other people to think highly of us. But when we see only the good things about ourselves, and we cannot see our sins and faults, then we are in trouble. Sometimes it is hard to ask God to forgive us for our sins because we can't think of our sins. We think that everything we do is wonderful. It was to people with this attitude (people like us) that Jesus told the following story.

Read—*Luke 18:9–14*

To some who were confident of their own righteousness and looked down on everybody else, Jesus told this parable: "Two men went up to the temple to pray, one a Pharisee and the other a tax collector. The Pharisee stood up and prayed about himself: 'God, I thank you that I am not like other men—robbers, evildoers, adulterers—or even like this tax collector. I fast twice a week and give a tenth of all I get.'

"But the tax collector stood at a distance. He would not even look up to heaven, but beat his breast and said, 'God, have mercy on me, a sinner.'

"I tell you that this man, rather than the other, went home justified before God. For everyone who exalts himself will be humbled, and he who humbles himself will be exalted."

Discuss

1. Describe the two men in Jesus' story. How were they alike? How were they different?
2. Which kind of prayer is easier to pray?
3. Which prayer did God like better?
4. What does it mean to humble oneself?

Final Thought

If we think we're perfect, we are only fooling ourselves. The truth is that we often think wrong thoughts and do wrong things that hurt other people, ourselves, and God. Pride also makes us think we have no need for God. No wonder God hates pride. Pride keeps us from being honest with ourselves, and it keeps us from receiving all that we need from God.

Pray

Dear Lord, have mercy on me, a sinner, for Jesus' sake.

Sing—*When I Survey the Wondrous Cross*

Forbid it, Lord, that I should boast
Save in the death of Christ, my God;
All the vain things that charm me most,
I sacrifice them to his blood.

Do

Place the symbol of the praying hands on your holiday tree.

Further Study for Adults

Read Matthew 6:1–8. Trace Jesus' use of the following words in this passage: seen, secret, reward. What point is Jesus making about our motivation, our approach, and our reward for good deeds? How is this similar to the teaching of the parable of the Pharisee and the tax collector?

SATURDAY

WEEK ONE

Wouldn't it be nice to have answers for all our questions? Sometimes answers do not help us. There is a big difference between knowing what is right and being able to do what is right. I knew it was wrong to lie, but that did not keep me from doing it on several memorable occasions. At the moment, it seemed more important to stay out of trouble than to do what was right.

In today's story, a man asks Jesus a very important question. But the answer only makes him sad.

Read—*Luke 18:18–30*

A certain ruler asked him, "Good teacher, what must I do to inherit eternal life?"

"Why do you call me good?" Jesus answered. "No one is good—except God alone. You know the commandments: 'Do not commit adultery, do not murder, do not steal, do not give false testimony, honor your father and mother.'"

"All these I have kept since I was a boy," he said.

When Jesus heard this, he said to him, "You still lack one thing. Sell everything you have and give to the poor, and you will have treasure in heaven. Then come, follow me."

When he heard this, he became very sad, because he was a man of great wealth. Jesus looked at him and said, "How hard it is for the rich to enter the kingdom of God! Indeed, it is easier for a camel to go through the eye of a needle than for a rich man to enter the kingdom of God."

Those who heard this asked, "Who then can be saved?"

Jesus replied, "What is impossible with men is possible with God."

Peter said to him, "We have left all we had to follow you!"

"I tell you the truth," Jesus said to them, "no one who has left home or wife or brothers or parents or children for the sake of the kingdom of God will fail to receive many times as much in this age and, in the age to come, eternal life."

Discuss
1. What question did the ruler ask Jesus?
2. How did Jesus answer? Why did the man go away sad?
3. Why do you think Jesus told him to sell everything he had?
4. What in your life might hold you back from following Christ?

Final Thought
What is good? The ruler thought that he was good. Jesus said, "You're not good enough. Only God is good enough." We must see our need of a Savior. Only Jesus Christ, who was God himself, is good enough to make us right with God.

Pray
Dear Lord, don't let anything hold me back from following you. Thank you for saving me from my sin.

Sing—*When I Survey the Wondrous Cross*

When I survey the wondrous cross
On which the prince of glory died,
My richest gain I count but loss
And pour contempt on all my pride.

Do
Place the symbol of the camel on your holiday tree.

Further Study for Adults
Read Luke 18:1–8, 15–17. The parable of the persistent widow and the account of Jesus and the little children are grouped in Luke's gospel with the parable of the Pharisee and the tax collector and the incident with the rich ruler. What common themes unite these stories? How does Jesus contrast the values of the Kingdom with the values of this world?

Did you know that the forty days of Lent do not include the Sundays? Can you guess why that is? Lent is a time of thinking about Jesus' death. Every Sunday of the year, however, is a celebration of Jesus' resurrection. For that reason, we will spend each of the six Sundays during Lent looking at one of the resurrection stories. In this story something frightening happens at Jesus' tomb. Death frightens us because we really do not understand it. Kids like to scare each other by telling spooky stories about death. Although the women in this story are afraid (with good reason), their fears turn to excitement. Try to imagine what it was like for them as they visited the tomb early that morning.

Read—*Luke 24:1–12*

On the first day of the week, very early in the morning, the women took the spices they had prepared and went to the tomb. They found the stone rolled away from the tomb, but when they entered, they did not find the body of the Lord Jesus. While they were wondering about this, suddenly two men in clothes that gleamed like lightning stood beside them. In their fright the women bowed down with their faces to the ground, but the men said to them, "Why do you look for the living among the dead? He is not here; he has risen! Remember how he told you, while he was still with you in Galilee: 'The Son of Man must be delivered into the hands of sinful men, be crucified and on the third day be raised again.'" Then they remembered his words.

When they came back from the tomb, they told all these things to the Eleven and to all the others. It was Mary Magdalene, Joanna, Mary the mother of James, and the others with them who told this to the apostles. But they did not believe the women, because their words seemed to them like nonsense. Peter, however, got up and ran to the tomb. Bending over, he saw the strips of linen lying by themselves, and he went away, wondering to himself what had happened.

Discuss

1. What did the women expect to see and do at the tomb?
2. What did they find instead?
3. What was their reaction?
4. How do you think they felt when the disciples did not believe them?

Final Thought

These women loved Jesus very much. They followed him and cared for him during his life, watched and wept as he died on the cross, and continued to be faithful to him in his death by bringing spices for his body. Unlike the disciples, these women did not disown Jesus or run away for fear when Jesus was arrested. Isn't it fitting, then, that they were the first ones to know about the resurrection?

Pray

Dear Lord, thank you for your resurrection. Help us to be like these women who were faithful to you no matter what.

Sing—*Christ the Lord Is Risen Today; Alleluia!*

Christians, on this holy day, Alleluia!
All your grateful homage pay; Alleluia!
Christ the Lord is ris'n on high; Alleluia!
Now he lives, no more to die. Alleluia!

Do

Place the symbol of the jar of spices on your holiday tree.

Further Study for Adults

Read Romans 6:5–11. According to this passage, what difference do Christ's death and resurrection make in our lives? What does it mean to count oneself dead to sin and alive to God in Christ Jesus (v. 10)? As far as God is concerned, because of Jesus' death and resurrection, we already are dead to sin and alive to him. How can we realize this in our present experience?

MONDAY

WEEK TWO

In today's story, a blind man does something which embarrasses some of Jesus' followers. Do you ever get embarrassed? I am not easily embarrassed. In fact, I am the kind of person who does things which others find embarrassing, particularly my kids. I love to sing, for instance, and sometimes I sing in places where singing is not what everyone else is doing. Most people don't sing in parking lots and shopping malls. My kids have gotten to the age where they care what other people think, so they do their best to hush me up.

I remember a time, however, when even I was embarrassed. It happened at a choir rehearsal which was held in an auditorium with seats that went down a sloping floor. On this particular evening, I had a miserable cold. Instead of tissues, I always carried a roll of toilet paper. In the middle of rehearsal, as I tried to pull off some toilet paper, the roll slipped out of my lap and shot down the sloping floor. People saw it as it whizzed by, and they turned to see where it came from. There I sat with the other end of the roll in my hand. It finally came out at the bottom row, in front of everyone. Do you remember an embarrassing incident from your past?

Read—*Luke 18:35–43*

As Jesus approached Jericho, a blind man was sitting by the roadside begging. When he heard the crowd going by, he asked what was happening. They told him, "Jesus of Nazareth is passing by."

He called out, "Jesus, Son of David, have mercy on me!"

Those who led the way rebuked him and told him to be quiet, but he shouted all the more, "Son of David, have mercy on me!"

Jesus stopped and ordered the man to be brought to him. When he came near, Jesus asked him, "What do you want me to do for you?"

"Lord, I want to see," he replied.

Jesus said to him, "Receive your sight; your faith has healed you." Immediately he received his sight and followed Jesus, praising God. When all the people saw it, they also praised God.

Discuss
1. What did the blind man do when he heard that Jesus was passing by?
2. When people told him to be quiet, what did he do? Why?
3. What was Jesus' response to the man?
4. Often we are like the followers who were embarrassed by the blind man. We care too much what others think. When can we be more bold in our faith?

Final Thought

Jesus was not embarrassed by the blind man's loud cries. He loved to see faith like that of the blind man, bold and persistent. It was a faith that (1) didn't care what others thought, (2) directly admitted his need, and (3) followed Jesus immediately and gladly, with a heart full of praise.

Pray

Dear Lord Jesus Christ, grow in us a faith like the blind man had. Help us not to be afraid but to trust in you and follow you gladly.

Sing—*My Faith Looks Up to Thee*

My faith looks up to thee, Thou Lamb of Calvary,
Saviour divine!
Now hear me while I pray, Take all my guilt away,
O let me from this day Be wholly thine.

Do

Place the symbol of eyes on your holiday tree.

Further Study for Adults

Read Matthew 22:41–45. What did the term "Son of David" mean? Why do you think the blind man cried out loudly to Jesus specifically calling him "Son of David?" What aspect of the blind man's faith most inspires you?

TUESDAY

WEEK TWO

Several years ago, Mark's watch disappeared. He set it down outside during an activity at school, and when he returned to get it, it was gone. I threw a fit and insisted that Mark find the watch. During the month that followed, there was much talk among the kids at school as to who took Mark's watch. Finally, the school counselor announced that if it were returned, there would be no punishment, no questions asked. Mark's watch was returned.

Have you ever taken something that didn't belong to you? All of us have, if we are honest with ourselves. Perhaps you tucked something in your pocket from a store or a friend's house. Or you took someone else's answer on a test in school. Mom or Dad, maybe you used your company's photocopier for personal copies, or reported that you had worked just a little bit longer than you really had. It is very easy to begin to steal in little ways. That is probably what happened to the man in today's story.

Read—*Luke 19:1–10*

Jesus entered Jericho and was passing through. A man was there by the name of Zacchaeus; he was a chief tax collector and was wealthy. He wanted to see who Jesus was, but being a short man he could not, because of the crowd. So he ran ahead and climbed a sycamore-fig tree to see him, since Jesus was coming that way.

When Jesus reached the spot, he looked up and said to him, "Zacchaeus, come down immediately. I must stay at your house today." So he came down at once and welcomed him gladly.

All the people saw this and began to mutter, "He has gone to be the guest of a 'sinner.'"

But Zacchaeus stood up and said to the Lord, "Look, Lord! Here and now I give half of my possessions to the poor, and if I have cheated anybody out of anything, I will pay back four times the amount."

Jesus said to him, "Today salvation has come to this house, because this man, too, is a son of Abraham. For the Son of Man came to seek and to save what was lost."

Discuss

1. What do we learn about Zacchaeus from these verses?
2. Why do you think Zacchaeus wanted to see Jesus?
3. How did the other people feel when Jesus invited himself over to Zacchaeus' house? Why?
4. How did Zacchaeus show that he loved Jesus?

Final Thought

Zacchaeus showed his faith by what he did. First, he wanted to see Jesus so badly that he climbed up in a tree. Then, when Jesus told him to come down and bring him home for dinner, Zacchaeus gladly obeyed. Jesus didn't tell Zacchaeus to pay back the money he had taken from people before he would come to his house. Jesus loved and accepted Zacchaeus just as he was. Jesus knew that when Zacchaeus spent a little time with him, he would want to make things right. And Zacchaeus did. That was the final way Zacchaeus showed that he loved and trusted the Lord.

Pray

Dear Lord, thank you for loving and accepting me just as I am. Help me to obey you gladly, as Zacchaeus did.

Sing—*Just as I Am*

Just as I am, and waiting not
To rid my soul of one dark blot,
To thee, whose Blood can cleanse each spot,
O Lamb of God, I come.

Do

Place the symbol of the branch from a tree on your holiday tree.

Further Study for Adults

Reflect on Zacchaeus' honesty and willingness to make personal sacrifice in order to set things right. These are two sure signs of a heart where Jesus resides. How is Christ's presence in your life making a practical difference?

When I was eleven, I discovered too late that it was my best friend's birthday. I wanted to give her something, but I couldn't get to the store. Because we both loved to read, I went to my bookshelves and pulled out my favorite book, one that had been my mother's. It was so old that the pages were hard and yellow. I could never replace that book. But because I loved my friend, I gave her my precious book. If you were to give a friend a gift of something that belonged to you, something very important to you that you could not replace, what would it be? What would cause you to give such a gift? Let's read about someone who gave an expensive gift to Jesus.

Read—*John 12:1–10*

Six days before the Passover, Jesus arrived at Bethany, where Lazarus lived, whom Jesus had raised from the dead. Here a dinner was given in Jesus' honor. Martha served, while Lazarus was among those reclining at the table with him. Then Mary took about a pint of pure nard, an expensive perfume; she poured it on Jesus' feet and wiped his feet with her hair. And the house was filled with the fragrance of the perfume.

But one of his disciples, Judas Iscariot, who was later to betray him, objected, "Why wasn't this perfume sold and the money given to the poor? It was worth a year's wages." He did not say this because he cared about the poor but because he was a thief; as keeper of the money bag, he used to help himself to what was put into it.

"Leave her alone," Jesus replied. "It was intended that she should save this perfume for the day of my burial. You will always have the poor among you, but you will not always have me."

Meanwhile a large crowd of Jews found out that Jesus was there and came, not only because of him but also to see Lazarus, whom he had raised from the dead. So the chief priests made plans to kill Lazarus as well, for on account of him many of the Jews were going over to Jesus and putting their faith in him.

Discuss

1. Martha, Mary, and Lazarus decided to give a dinner party for Jesus, probably celebrating how Jesus raised Lazarus from the dead. Who was at the party?
2. Why do you think Mary poured her expensive perfume on Jesus' feet and wiped his feet with her hair?
3. Who got angry about this? Why?
4. What did Jesus say?

Final Thought

Jesus accepted Mary's love gift and defended her before Judas. When we truly love Jesus and give ourselves completely to him, as Mary did, we will come up against criticism. We must pay no attention to the Judases. Only Jesus' opinion matters.

Pray

Thank you, Lord Jesus, for loving me so much that you went to the cross for me. Help me to love you as Mary did.

Sing—*Jesus, Priceless Treasure*

Jesus, priceless treasure, Source of purest pleasure,
Truest friend to me: Ah, how long I've panted,
And my heart has fainted, Thirsting, Lord, for thee!
Thine I am, O spotless Lamb;
I will suffer nought to hide thee, Nought I ask beside thee.

Do

Place the symbol of the perfume bottle on your holiday tree.

Further Study for Adults

Read John 11:1–57. This chapter immediately precedes today's passage about Christ's anointing at Bethany. What does John 11 show us about Mary's personality and her relationship with Jesus? Why was this miracle so controversial? The more realistically we see Jesus, the less "safe, middle ground" we find. Either we must embrace him with our whole selves, as Mary did, or we must be his enemies.

THURSDAY

WEEK TWO

It may seem odd to be reading about Palm Sunday when that is still weeks away. But so many things happened during that last week before Jesus' death and resurrection, that we want to take our time. So for the next few days we will pretend that it is Palm Sunday.

In these verses, Jesus borrows something. Do you ever borrow things? Sometimes Mark and Laura forget their lunches at home and they have to borrow money for the school lunch. They usually pay back the money right away.

My friend Jeannie recently had a college-age man staying at her home. She and her husband let him borrow one of their cars. Within the first week, he got a ticket for speeding and a few days later, he wrecked their car. My friends were generous to lend this young man their car, but he proved that he was not worthy of their trust.

Have you ever lent something to someone who ruined it or never returned it? You probably didn't lend anything to that person again. Being responsible and trustworthy makes a big difference. People will lend things much more readily to those whom they trust. And Jesus was just such a person.

Read—*Luke 19:28–35*

After Jesus had said this, he went on ahead, going up to Jerusalem. As he approached Bethphage and Bethany at the hill called the Mount of Olives, he sent two of his disciples, saying to them, "Go to the village ahead of you, and as you enter it, you will find a colt tied there, which no one has ever ridden. Untie it and bring it here. If anyone asks you, 'Why are you untying it?' tell him, 'The Lord needs it.'"

Those who were sent ahead went and found it just as he had told them. As they were untying the colt, its owners asked them, "Why are you untying the colt?"

They replied, "The Lord needs it."

They brought it to Jesus, threw their cloaks on the colt and put Jesus on it.

Discuss

1. On what mission did Jesus send two of his disciples?
2. What did Jesus know about the colt? How do you think he knew these things?
3. When the disciples found the colt, what happened?
4. Why do you think the owners let the disciples take the colt?

Final Thought

Sometimes the Lord calls us to do something, yet we still worry about how it will all work out. When we worry, we are not really believing that Jesus is God and that he loves us. You see, Jesus knew all about the colt and how his Father in heaven had prepared that colt for him. In the same way, when Jesus asks us to do something, he has everything prepared in advance for us. All we have to do is trust and obey his Word.

Pray

Dear Lord, thank you that you prepare the way before us. Help us always to walk in your way, trusting and obeying you.

Sing—*If You But Trust in God to Guide You*

Sing, pray, and keep his ways unswerving;
Offer your service faithfully,
And trust his word; though undeserving,
You'll find his promise true to be.
God never will forsake in need
The soul that trusts in him indeed.

Do

Place the symbol of a colt on your holiday tree.

Further Study for Adults

Read Zechariah 9:9. When Jesus determined to enter Jerusalem riding on a colt, what significance did it have to the Jews? Why do you think he did this?

FRIDAY

WEEK TWO

Have you ever wanted to be a star? Most of us, at one time or another, dream of a moment of glory. Those who play sports dream of making the winning shot in the championship game or receiving the gold medal in the Olympics. Those who enjoy music dream of a standing ovation at Carnegie Hall—in their honor.

Most of us dream about such a moment—a time when everyone's admiration and attention focus on us. For many of us, our wedding is our "big moment." I remember well walking down the church aisle on my father's arm to the music of the pipe organ. My dad was overcome with emotion—happy for me, yet sad that he was losing his "little girl." People turned and craned their necks to get a glimpse of the bride. Friends and loved ones beamed with joy on my behalf. I had hardly dared to dream that such a wonderful thing would happen to me! But there I was in a veil and flowing white dress, with the man I loved waiting for me at the front of the church! It was a tender, glorious moment, one I will never forget.

In today's verses, Jesus is at the center of attention. In many ways, Jesus' entrance into Jerusalem is like a wedding march. As you read, think about how the crowd showed that they were excited about Jesus. Also, think about how Jesus reacted to the attention.

Read—*Luke 19:36–40*

As he went along, people spread their cloaks on the road.

When he came near the place where the road goes down the Mount of Olives, the whole crowd of disciples began joyfully to praise God in loud voices for all the miracles they had seen:

"Blessed is the king who comes in the name of the Lord!"

"Peace in heaven and glory in the highest!"

Some of the Pharisees in the crowd said to Jesus, "Teacher, rebuke your disciples!"

"I tell you," he replied, "if they keep quiet, the stones will cry out."

Discuss
1. How did the people show their excitement?
2. Why were they so excited about Jesus?
3. How did Jesus feel about being praised?
4. Why do you think the Pharisees told Jesus to make everybody stop? What did Jesus mean by his reply?

Final Thought
Jesus' entry into Jerusalem was different than a wedding in that a happy marriage did not await him. Instead, he was riding to his death. Jesus knew very well that these crowds would soon desert him in his darkest hour. He knew that they loved him for what they thought he would give them—not for who he truly was. Yet he didn't turn away their praise. He accepted it graciously, for only he, the eternal Son of God, is worthy of praise and worship.

Pray
Dear Lord, help us to love you, not for what you give us, but for who you are. Accept our feeble attempts at worship today.

Sing—*All Glory, Laud, and Honor*

All glory, laud, and honor To you, redeemer, king,
To whom the lips of children Made sweet hosannas ring.
You are the king of Israel And David's royal Son,
Now in the Lord's Name coming, Our King and Blessed One!

Do
Place the symbol of a coat on your holiday tree.

Further Study for Adults
Read Matthew 21:8–17. What additional details are included in this account? What part did children play? Jesus quoted Psalm 8:2 in response to the Jewish leaders' objections. This must have really irked them, for Psalm 8:2 refers to praise of God, and here Jesus applies it to himself. The innocent, heart-felt praise of children had a real impact.

SATURDAY

WEEK TWO

I have a friend, Rachel, who went through a very painful divorce several years ago. Rachel's mother died shortly after she was married, about fifteen years prior to her divorce. I never knew Rachel's mom, but everyone loved and admired her. She was a godly woman who loved the Lord with her whole heart. Folks tell me that she poured out her life for others—family, friends, and her little country church. Rachel thought the world of her mother and grieved her loss deeply. Since her divorce, however, Rachel says to me, "I'm so glad that my mother wasn't living to see me go through this. It would have hurt her so."

God knew what he was doing when he did not reveal the future to us. Knowledge of tomorrow's difficulties is too great a burden for today. It is so much better for us to trust God for one day at a time.

Because Jesus was God, he did know the future. He knew the dreadful things that would soon happen to him. In these verses we see that he knew what horrible things would happen to Jerusalem, the holy city, and the people who lived there. Jesus' words were fulfilled less than forty years later, when the Romans seized Jerusalem by building an embankment around the city. Many Jewish men, women, and children died in this attack. The walls and the temple were destroyed, and much of Jerusalem lay in ruins. And more disasters would follow for the "City of Peace."

Read—*Luke 19:41–44*

As he approached Jerusalem and saw the city, he wept over it and said, "If you, even you, had only known on this day what would bring you peace—but now it is hidden from your eyes. The days will come upon you when your enemies will build an embankment against you and encircle you and hem you in on every side. They will dash you to the ground, you and the children within your walls. They will not leave one stone on another, because you did not recognize the time of God's coming to you."

Discuss
1. What did Jesus do when he saw Jerusalem?
2. Jesus had been to Jerusalem many other times. Why did he cry this time?
3. What did Jesus say would happen to Jerusalem?
4. In verse 44, Jesus told why these terrible things were to take place. What was the reason?

Final Thought
If I had been treated the way Jesus was treated by the Jewish leaders, I would have wanted revenge, I'm afraid. Yet Jesus did not want revenge. He did not want judgment to fall on Jerusalem. He wanted them to experience peace. This is a perfect example of what Jesus taught, that we should bless those who curse us. He loved and wanted the best for those who hurt and killed him.

Pray
Dear Lord, help me to be more like you, to care deeply for others—even for those who hurt me. Thank you for loving me and forgiving me when I do things that hurt you.

Sing—*My Song Is Love Unknown*

He came from his blest throne Salvation to bestow;
But men made strange, and none The longed-for Christ would know.
But O, my friend, my friend indeed,
Who at my need His life should spend.

Do
Place the symbol of a stone on your holiday tree.

Further Study for Adults
Read Matthew 5:43–48. How did Jesus exemplify these verses? Are there current political leaders or personal enemies in whose downfall you would delight? What steps can you take today to begin to love them as Jesus did his enemies?

SUNDAY

SECOND SUNDAY IN LENT

Today is the Lord's Day, a celebration of the resurrection, and once again we will take another glimpse at that glorious day that Jesus was resurrected from the dead. The verses that we will read today are about a race. My friend Linda enjoys running in races. One year she ran in the Marine Corps marathon. I enjoy race-walking more than running. One of my favorite things to do is to go for a nice brisk walk with a good friend. I like the combination of exercise, fresh air, and conversation.

Do you ever run races with your friends? Several years ago, Laura came home from school smiling proudly and boasting, "I can run faster than anyone in my class! When I run, none of the boys can catch me!" We were amused to hear that and wondered how many years it would be before Laura wanted the boys to catch her! Sometimes we run for the fun of running, and sometimes we run because we want to get someplace in a hurry. See if you can figure out why the people in these verses were running.

Read—*John 20:1–9*

Early on the first day of the week, while it was still dark, Mary Magdalene went to the tomb and saw that the stone had been removed from the entrance. So she came running to Simon Peter and the other disciple, the one Jesus loved, and said, "They have taken the Lord out of the tomb, and we don't know where they have put him!"

So Peter and the other disciple started for the tomb. Both were running, but the other disciple outran Peter and reached the tomb first. He bent over and looked in at the strips of linen lying there but did not go in. Then Simon Peter, who was behind him, arrived and went into the tomb. He saw the strips of linen lying there, as well as the burial cloth that had been around Jesus' head. The cloth was folded up by itself, separate from the linen. Finally the other disciple, who had reached the tomb first, also went inside. He saw and believed. (They still did not understand from Scripture that Jesus had to rise from the dead.)

Discuss
1. John, who is the writer, refers to himself here as "the other disciple." Why did he and Peter race to the tomb?
2. Who arrived first? Who entered the tomb first?
3. What did they see when they entered the tomb?
4. What do you think it means that John "saw and believed"?

Final Thought
Why do you suppose John included so many details in his account? I can think of two reasons. First, John was there himself and was writing exactly what he remembered. Sometimes when important things happen to us, it is the tiny details that stand out in our minds. Second, John wanted his readers to know that what he was writing was true, so that they would also believe that Jesus was risen from the dead. Giving a detailed account proved that John was there and had seen these things with his own eyes.

Pray
Dear Lord Jesus, thank you that you truly rose from the dead. Because you did, we know that you are the only Savior and Lord.

Sing—*Christ the Lord is Risen Today; Alleluia!*

Christ the Lord is ris'n today; Alleluia!
Christians, hasten on your way; Alleluia!
Offer praise with love replete, Alleluia!
At the paschal victim's feet. Alleluia!

Do
Place the symbol of a running shoe on your holiday tree.

Further Study for Adults
Read Acts 2:22–32. These words are spoken by Peter. Peter claims that Jesus fulfilled Psalm 16:8–11 in his resurrection. What does that prove? How does the fact that Peter was a witness help his case? Does the veracity of the resurrection make a difference in our lives? As we witness to unbelievers?

MONDAY

WEEK THREE

Several weeks ago our car was vandalized while we were in church. We came out to find one of the windshield wipers bent up—totally ruined. That was not what we expected to find when we came out of church! It made me so angry! I couldn't understand how someone could find pleasure in destroying someone else's property. Jim was angry, too, but he was not surprised. He reminded me that we live in world full of sinful people. The surprise is that these things do not happen more often than they do. Even so, I was still angry. I had to go to the auto parts store and buy a new wiper, which Jim and Mark installed. (Fortunately, Jim is very handy with cars, so we did not have to pay for the repair.) I also went to the police station and filed a report. But it wasn't the expense or inconvenience that bothered me, for these were minimal. It was the sense that someone had not respected my property. I could no longer park in that parking garage for fear that a similar problem—or worse—might occur. And that too made me mad.

The day after Jesus entered Jerusalem on the donkey, he went to the temple to teach and to worship his Father. What he saw when he got there made him very angry, too.

Read—*Mark 11:15–19*

On reaching Jerusalem, Jesus entered the temple area and began driving out those who were buying and selling there. He overturned the tables of the money changers and the benches of those selling doves, and would not allow anyone to carry merchandise through the temple courts. And as he taught them, he said, "Is it not written:
'My house will be called
a house of prayer for all nations'?
But you have made it 'a den of robbers.'"

The chief priests and the teachers of the law heard this and began looking for a way to kill him, for they feared him, because the whole crowd was amazed at his teaching.

When evening came, they went out of the city.

Discuss

1. What did Jesus find when he entered the temple?
2. What did he do about it?
3. Why do you think this made Jesus so angry?
4. How did the people react to Jesus?

Final Thought

Three things were wrong here. First, the sellers were charging too much for the animals for sacrifices. Second, this was taking place in the part of the temple that was the place for Gentiles (non-Jews) to worship God. How could they possibly worship amidst all this commotion? Third, and most important, they were treating God's place of worship with disrespect. And that meant that they were not treating God with respect. Jesus got angry because people were not being treated right and God was not being honored. Those are good reasons to be angry.

Pray

Dear Lord, often when I am angry it is because I feel I haven't been treated fairly. Forgive me. Help me to be more concerned with respecting others and honoring you.

Sing—*Rock of Ages*

Not the labors of my hands can fulfill thy law's demands;
Could my zeal no respite know, could my tears forever flow,
All for sin could not atone; Thou must save, and thou alone.

Do

Place the symbol of the table on your holiday tree.

Further Study for Adults

Reflect on anger and its place in our lives, according to Scripture. Read Ephesians 4:26 and James 1:19–20. When is anger pure and when does it become sinful? Is there anger in your heart that should not be harbored? Is there passivity where there should be anger?

Some of the stories I have written have made people upset. Usually they were upset because they saw themselves in my story, and they did not like what I had written about them. Here is a story that Jesus told just a few days before his arrest. It was not a pleasant, fun story. Rather it was a story which made some upset and made others very angry.

Read—*Luke 20:9–19*

He went on to tell the people this parable: "A man planted a vineyard, rented it to some farmers and went away for a long time. At harvest time he sent a servant to the tenants so they would give him some of the fruit of the vineyard. But the tenants beat him and sent him away empty-handed. He sent another servant, but that one also they beat and treated shamefully and sent away empty-handed. He sent still a third, and they wounded him and threw him out.

"Then the owner of the vineyard said, 'What shall I do? I will send my son, whom I love; perhaps they will respect him.'

"But when the tenants saw him, they talked the matter over. 'This is the heir,' they said. 'Let's kill him, and the inheritance will be ours.' So they threw him out of the vineyard and killed him.

"What then will the owner of the vineyard do to them? He will come and kill those tenants and give the vineyard to others."

When the people heard this, they said, "May this never be!"

Jesus looked directly at them and asked, "Then what is the meaning of that which is written:

"'The stone which the builders rejected has become the capstone'?

Everyone who falls on that stone will be broken to pieces, but he on whom it falls will be crushed."

The teachers of the law and the chief priests looked for a way to arrest him immediately, because they knew he had spoken this parable against them. But they were afraid of the people.

Discuss

1. What happened to the servants that the owner sent to collect some of the fruit?
2. Then whom did the owner send? What did the tenants do to him?
3. This story was like a secret code. Jesus was giving a message to the people who were planning to kill him. Can you figure out the meaning of the story?
4. Who understood Jesus' meaning? How did they react?

Final Thought

What made the Jewish leaders so angry was that Jesus was claiming to be the Son of God. They did not want to believe that. If we tell others the truth about Jesus, some will become very angry, just like the Jewish leaders. Most people do not want to believe that Jesus Christ is the only way to God. They want to think that they are good enough on their own.

Pray

Dear Lord, give me courage to tell others about you, even if they don't like what I say. Help me to be loving and truthful.

Sing—*Jesus, Priceless Treasure*

In thine arm I rest me; Foes who would molest me
Cannot reach me here. Though the earth be shaking,
Every heart be quaking, Jesus calms my fear.
Sin and hell in conflict fell
With their bitter storms assail me, Jesus will not fail me.

Do

Place the symbol of the grapevine on your holiday tree.

Further Study for Adults

Reflect on verses. 17–18. Jesus is quoting Psalm 118:22. What does this mean, and why did Jesus say this to the leaders?

Has anyone ever tricked you or played a joke on you? How did you feel? When I was a teenager, the boys at my church loved to tease me. They knew that I would be a good sport and go along with it, making everyone laugh. One boy in particular, Steve, loved to torment me. If I woke up to find toilet paper streaming down from the branches of the trees in my yard, I knew that Steve was behind the prank. It was all in good fun. As I cleaned up the mess, I planned my revenge. This rivalry went on for years.

Sometimes, however, people play tricks to be mean. They don't care if they hurt someone, just so long as they have a laugh. I remember such a situation from my junior high days. I had a friend named Mary who was homely and somewhat mentally handicapped. One day she showed me a note that she had received. It was a love letter from one of the popular boys. Her eyes sparkled with excitement. Carefully I tried to explain to her that she probably shouldn't take the note too seriously. Later that day, when Mary wasn't around, I told the boy just what I thought of his mean trick.

In today's reading, the Jewish leaders try to trick Jesus.

Read—*Luke 20:20–26*

Keeping a close watch on him, they sent spies, who pretended to be honest. They hoped to catch Jesus in something he said so that they might hand him over to the power and authority of the governor. So the spies questioned him: "Teacher, we know that you speak and teach what is right, and that you do not show partiality but teach the way of God in accordance with the truth. Is it right for us to pay taxes to Caesar or not?"

He saw through their duplicity and said to them, "Show me a denarius. Whose portrait and inscription are on it?"

"Caesar's," they replied.

He said to them, "Then give to Caesar what is Caesar's, and to God what is God's."

They were unable to trap him in what he had said there in public. And astonished by his answer, they became silent.

Discuss
1. Why were the Jewish leaders trying to trick Jesus?
2. What question did the spies ask Jesus?
3. How was this question meant to trap Jesus?
4. Explain Jesus' answer.

Final Thought
This question was meant to force Jesus to take sides with either the Jews or the Romans. Jesus' answer said, "You have a responsibility to Caesar and you have a responsibility to God." He refused to take sides. Instead he taught that each person must be responsible for obeying God and earthly leaders. People today try to trap Jesus. We want Jesus to be on our side, to answer our prayers just the way we want them to be answered. But the question is not, Whose side is Jesus on? The question is, Are we on his side? Will we do whatever he tells us to do?

Pray
Dear Lord, forgive us for all the times we try to get you to do or say the things we want. Help us to live for you.

Sing—*Rock of Ages*

Nothing in my hand I bring, Simply to thy Cross I cling;
Naked, come to thee for dress; Helpless, look to thee for grace;
Foul, I to the fountain fly; Wash me, Savior, or I die.

Do
Place the symbol of a dollar bill on your holiday tree.

Further Study for Adults
Reflect on the message of Jesus' words in this incident. What is Jesus saying about money? What is he saying about responsibility? Values? What are the implications for your life?

Laura is a safety patrol, and yesterday afternoon the patrols had their end of the school year party. They played bingo, and the winners were awarded wonderful canteens as prizes. In the second to the last round, two girls tied as winners, so the teacher give both of them a canteen. Laura won the last round, but they had run out of canteens, so she came away with no prize at all. Through tears she told me that everyone else had won prizes during the course of the year. This was the very first time she won a game—and she still didn't get a prize. She ached with disappointment. It just didn't seem fair!

"That's not fair!" We've all said these words at one time or another. Whether at home, in the neighborhood, at school, or at work, most of us have experienced the frustration of being misunderstood or treated unfairly. We should not expect things to be fair, because we live in a world of sin. If you think about it, most people in the world would look at us and complain "that's not fair!" because we are so much better off than they are.

But that does not give us an excuse to treat people unfairly. God calls us to go beyond fairness. Let's see what Jesus had to say about these groups of people and their importance to God.

Read—Luke 20:45–21:4

While all the people were listening, Jesus said to his disciples, "Beware of the teachers of the law. They like to walk around in flowing robes and love to be greeted in the marketplaces and have the most important seats in the synagogues and the places of honor at banquets. They devour widows' houses and for a show make lengthy prayers. Such men will be punished most severely."

As he looked up, Jesus saw the rich putting their gifts into the temple treasury. He also saw a poor widow put in two very small copper coins. "I tell you the truth," he said, "this poor widow has put in more than all the others. All these people gave their gifts out of their wealth; but she out of her poverty put in all she had to live on."

Discuss
1. How did Jesus describe the teachers of the law?
2. Why did he warn people to watch out for them?
3. What did Jesus see at the temple?
4. Why was the widow's gift more valuable than the rich people's gifts?

Final Thought
What is important to God is just the opposite of what is considered important in this world. Even Christians have fallen into the trap of the world's values. We run after Christian celebrities the same way the world runs after Hollywood movie stars. Jesus calls us to value those who have it hard in this life. We must love and help them, and treat them with honor.

Pray
Dear Lord Jesus, thank you for caring for the people who are not valued in this world. Help me to be like the widow, giving from my heart, and not like the leaders, doing things for show.

Sing—*When I Survey the Wondrous Cross*

Were the whole realm of nature mine,
That were an offering far too small;
Love so amazing, so divine,
Demands my soul, my life, my all.

Do
Place the symbol of two pennies on your holiday tree.

Further Study for Adults
Reflect on your life and your values. How have you embraced the world's value system, even in the context of the church? Can you think of people you know who are like the widow in today's passage? What can you do this week to begin to honor and uphold these folks?

FRIDAY

WEEK THREE

There is a girl in my daughter Laura's class who is mean to Laura. They used to be friends, although not close friends. Sybil is as nice as can be when the teacher is looking, but when no adults are around, she sticks her tongue out at Laura, or says nasty things to her under her breath. She tells other girls not to be Laura's friend.

Has this ever happened to you? It hurts even more when you are betrayed by a close friend. Mark experienced this several years ago. He developed a friendship with a nice boy named David who was already good friends with another boy, Rodney. David and Rodney had a secret club, with all sorts of rules and regulations. They let Mark join, and Mark was delighted. But Rodney apparently was not too thrilled with the new arrangement. He didn't want to share David's friendship. Suddenly Mark found that the two of them sided against him, expelling him from the club for one reason or another. David was nice to Mark when the two of them were alone. When Rodney was there too, however, David seemed to turn against Mark. Eventually Rodney learned that Mark would not "take David away from him." Things seemed to straighten out after a while. But there were some painful moments during the process.

Jesus knows exactly how we feel when we have been betrayed. Today we read about a close friend of Jesus, who decided to become his enemy.

Read—*Luke 22:1–6*

Now the Feast of Unleavened Bread, called the Passover, was approaching, and the chief priests and the teachers of the law were looking for some way to get rid of Jesus, for they were afraid of the people. Then Satan entered Judas, called Iscariot, one of the Twelve. And Judas went to the chief priests and the officers of the temple guard and discussed with them how he might betray Jesus. They were delighted and agreed to give him money. He consented, and watched for an opportunity to hand Jesus over to them when no crowd was present.

Discuss

1. What were the chief priests and teachers of the law trying to do? Why?
2. What happened to Judas that made him go to the chief priests?
3. How do you think Satan got control over Judas?
4. After Judas made the agreement, what did he start doing?

Final Thought

Judas used his position as one of the disciples to bring harm to Jesus and to get money for himself. There is no excuse for Judas' action. He allowed Satan to gain control over his heart and mind. His little agreement with the priests was a plot hatched in hell. Watch out for people like Judas, people who have no love in them, who think only of themselves and of money. And if you find that you are becoming like Judas, ask God to forgive you and to give you a new heart.

Prayer

Dear Lord, we are sorry for loving ourselves more than we love you. Forgive us and cleanse us. Make us new.

Sing—*Beneath the Cross of Jesus*

Upon the Cross of Jesus, Mine eye at times can see
The very dying form of One Who suffered there for me;
And from my smitten heart, with tears, Two wonders I confess:
The wonder of his glorious love, And my own worthlessness.

Do

Place the symbol of the black heart on your treasure table.

Further Study for Adults

Read John 13:13–30. This scene takes place during the Last Supper. What do these verses reveal about Judas and Jesus? Judas was evidently sitting close to Jesus, possibly at his right hand, the seat of honor. What is Jesus' attitude toward his betrayer?

When you have a big celebration at your house, do you have to make any preparations? If you said no, just ask your mom or dad!

The celebration for which Jesus and his disciples were preparing was the Passover meal. This was one of the most important days of the year for the Jews. God commanded them to celebrate it every year so that they would always remember how he had delivered them out of Pharaoh's hand, out of bondage in Egypt.

In the Passover meal, each item of food has a special meaning. Parsley dipped in salt water stands for the life of pain and tears that the Israelites lived when they were slaves in Egypt. The matzah, or unleavened bread, is eaten to remind us that the Israelites had to flee quickly that night. They could not wait for their bread to rise.

This meal takes a little bit of preparation. When Jesus and his disciples celebrated Passover, they too needed to make preparations. To learn more about that celebration and how God told them to observe it, it would be helpful to read about the first Passover meal in Exodus 12. Parents of young children, you may want to read it on your own and summarize it for your children in simple terms.

Read—Luke 22:7–13

Then came the day of Unleavened Bread on which the Passover lamb had to be sacrificed. Jesus sent Peter and John, saying, "Go and make preparations for us to eat the Passover."

"Where do you want us to prepare for it?" they asked.

He replied, "As you enter the city, a man carrying a jar of water will meet you. Follow him to the house that he enters, and say to the owner of the house, 'The Teacher asks: Where is the guest room, where I may eat the Passover with my disciples?' He will show you a large upper room, all furnished. Make preparations there."

They left and found things just as Jesus had told them. So they prepared the Passover.

Discuss

1. Think about the Passover meal. What preparations needed to be made?
2. How did the disciples know where to prepare for the meal?
3. The man carrying the jar of water is a mystery. Who do you think he was? Do you think Jesus had spoken to him ahead of time? (We can only guess.)
4. What do we learn about Jesus from these verses?

Final Thought

Special occasions require thoughtful preparation. Just as Jesus and the disciples made preparations for celebrating the Passover, the staff and clergy of your church spend many hours preparing for each worship service. Let us show thanks for all who work hard so that our worship may be meaningful.

Pray

Dearest Lord, thank you that you care about all the details of our lives. Help us to follow you in all our plans and preparations.

Sing—*Jesus, the Very Thought of You*

Jesus, the very thought of you
Fills us with sweet delight;
But sweeter far your face to view
And rest within your light.

Do

Place the symbol of the water jug on your holiday tree.

Further Study for Adults

Read Proverbs 3:5,6 and 16:9. What do these verses teach about making plans? What does it mean to "acknowledge him" in all your ways? In what areas of your life do you need God's direction now? How can you apply the truths of these verses to these areas of your life?

SUNDAY

THIRD SUNDAY IN LENT

Our friend Martha Vetter, who lives with us, almost lost her father a year ago. Dr. Vetter suffered a series of heart attacks, underwent heart surgery, then experienced a number of complications. Martha flew down to North Carolina to be with him. As she sat beside his bed, talking and praying with him, she thought that this might be her final conversation with her father. After that point, however, Dr. Vetter steadily improved. Martha truly felt that she had received her father back from death.

If you have ever had a family member almost die, you know the feelings of gratitude, relief, and joy that flood your soul when your loved one is restored to you. Death is so final. Never again can you hear that person's voice or feel his touch.

Read—*John 20:10–18*

Then the disciples went back to their homes, but Mary stood outside the tomb crying. As she wept, she bent over to look into the tomb and saw two angels in white, seated where Jesus' body had been, one at the head and the other at the foot.

They asked her, "Woman, why are you crying?"

"They have taken my Lord away," she said, "and I don't know where they have put him." At this, she turned around and saw Jesus standing there, but she did not realize that it was Jesus.

"Woman," he said, "why are you crying? Who is it you are looking for?"

Thinking he was the gardener, she said, "Sir, if you have carried him away, tell me where you have put him, and I will get him."

Jesus said to her, "Mary."

She turned toward him and cried out in Aramaic, "Rabboni!" (which means Teacher).

Jesus said, "Do not hold on to me, for I have not yet returned to the Father. Go instead to my brothers and tell them, 'I am returning to my Father and your Father, to my God and your God.'"

Mary Magdalene went to the disciples with the news: "I have seen the Lord!" And she told them that he had said these things to her.

Discuss

1. What was Mary doing outside Jesus' tomb? Why?
2. What did she see? Did she seem surprised? Why or why not?
3. Why do you suppose Mary did not at first recognize Jesus?
4. What do you think she felt when she heard him say her name?

Final thought

Mary Magdalene was the first person to see Jesus after the resurrection. Why did he first appear to her rather than Peter or John? Perhaps because she needed him the most. Once Mary's need was met, Jesus gave her an assignment. Others were hurting as well and needed to be told the good news.

Pray

Thank you, Lord Jesus, that you meet all my needs. Help me to share your good news with others who need you as well.

Sing—*Jesus Christ Is Risen Today*

Jesus Christ is ris'n today, Alleluia!
Our triumphant holy day, Alleluia!
Who did once upon the cross, Alleluia!
Suffer to redeem our loss. Alleluia!

Do

Place the symbol of the gardening spade on your holiday tree.

Further Study for Adults

Read Philippians 4:19. Write this verse in your own words. How has God kept this promise in your life thus far? What current needs can you offer to God? Who else needs to be reminded of God's glorious riches in Christ Jesus?

MONDAY

WEEK FOUR

Just before the Passover meal, a basin of water is passed around, and each person must wash their hands. This is to remind us that God requires that we come before him with pure hearts.

Read—*John 13:1–17*

It was just before the Passover Feast. Jesus knew that the time had come for him to leave this world and go to the Father. Having loved his own who were in the world, he now showed them the full extent of his love.

The evening meal was being served, and the devil had already prompted Judas Iscariot, son of Simon, to betray Jesus. Jesus knew that the Father had put all things under his power, and that he had come from God and was returning to God; so he got up from the meal, took off his outer clothing, and wrapped a towel around his waist. After that, he poured water into a basin and began to wash his disciples' feet, drying them with the towel that was wrapped around him.

He came to Simon Peter, who said to him, "Lord, are you going to wash my feet?"

Jesus replied, "You do not realize now what I am doing, but later you will understand."

"No," said Peter, "you shall never wash my feet."

Jesus answered, "A person who has had a bath needs only to wash his feet; his whole body is clean. And you are clean, though not every one of you." For he knew who was going to betray him, and that was why he said not every one was clean.

When he had finished washing their feet, he put on his clothes and returned to his place. "Do you understand what I have done for you?" he asked them. "You call me 'Teacher' and 'Lord,' and rightly so, for that is what I am. Now that I, your Lord and Teacher, have washed your feet, you also should wash one another's feet. I have set you an example that you should do as I have done for you. I tell you the truth, no servant is greater than his master, nor is a messenger greater than the one who sent him. Now that you know these things, you will be blessed if you do them."

Discuss
1. When dinner was served, what did Jesus do?
2. This was the job of the lowest servant. Why did Jesus do it?
3. Why didn't Peter want Jesus to wash his feet?
4. Are there things that we are not willing to do for others, especially members of our family? What attitude does Jesus want us to have?

Final Thought
Servanthood is not a popular idea these days. No one wants to be a doormat. Yet Jesus' example is bold and strong. No act of service is too small or dirty for him. Jesus showed us that there is nothing more powerful than the lifestyle of love through humble service for others.

Pray
Help me, Lord, to be willing to do the unpleasant and inconvenient things that love requires.

Sing—*The King of Love My Shepherd Is*

The King of love my shepherd is,
Whose goodness faileth never,
I nothing lack if I am his
And he is mine forever.

Do
Place the symbol of the towel on your holiday tree.

Further Study for Adults
Read Philippians 2:1–11. What was Christ's attitude and how was it shown? What do these verses teach us about our attitudes and actions in our relationships? Is there a particular relationship in your life which needs an attitude transformation? What can you do to cooperate with the Holy Spirit in this?

Have you ever been happy and sad at the same time? My parents were both happy and sad at my wedding. They were happy for me, that I was marrying such a wonderful man. But they were sad to lose their oldest daughter. In fact, when we left the church, we were on our way to our new home in Virginia, a thousand miles away from our families. That coming goodbye cast a shadow of sadness over our wedding. In fact, when we were planning the wedding, my mom slipped and referred to it as "the funeral."

Passover is a joyous celebration of God's goodness to his people. Yet as Jesus celebrated it with his disciples that night, he knew that soon his body would be broken and his blood shed, just as the matzah is broken and the cups of wine are poured in the *seder*. He knew that his friends would soon desert him, and one would betray him.

Read—Mark 14:17–26

When the evening came, Jesus arrived with the Twelve. While they were reclining at the table eating, he said, "I tell you the truth, one of you will betray me—one who is eating with me."

They were saddened, and one by one they said to him, "Surely not I?"

"It is one of the Twelve," he replied, "one who dips bread into the bowl with me. The Son of Man will go just as it is written about him. But woe to that man who betrays the Son of Man! It would be better for him if he had not been born."

While they were eating, Jesus took bread, gave thanks and broke it, and gave it to his disciples, saying, "Take it; this is my body."

Then he took the cup, gave thanks and offered it to them, and they all drank from it.

"This is my blood of the covenant, which is poured out for many," he said to them. "I tell you the truth, I will not drink again of the fruit of the vine until that day when I drink it anew in the kingdom of God."

When they had sung a hymn, they went out to the Mount of Olives.

Discuss

1. How was this meal different than the meals at your house?
2. What sad things did Jesus say at this supper?
3. What did Jesus say about the bread? the cup of wine?
4. How would you have felt if you had been one of the Twelve?

Final Thought

The wine and the matzot, or unleavened bread, were a very important part of the Passover celebration. Passover was the celebration of God's deliverance of the Jews from slavery in Egypt. When Jesus identified himself with the bread and the wine, he was telling his disciples, and us, that it would be by his death that we would be delivered from sin.

Pray

Dear Lord, we are sorry that we sin against you. Thank you for dying on the cross to deliver us from sin.

Sing—*I Lay My Sins on Jesus*

I lay my sins on Jesus, The spotless Lamb of God;
He bears them all and frees us From the accursed load.
I bring my guilt to Jesus To wash my crimson stains
Clean in his blood most precious Till not a spot remains.

Do

Place the symbol of the wine glass on your holiday tree.

Further Study for Adults

Read 1 Corinthians 11:23–34. What additional facts does this passage teach about the Last Supper? about the Lord's Supper in general? What do you think it means to eat and drink "in an unworthy manner"? What are we to remember as we partake of the Lord's Supper?

Yesterday I was driving my son Mark to the hardware store. I felt as if I were dragging lead weights around, I was so sluggish. Puzzled as to why I was so tired, I voiced some of my ideas to Mark. "Maybe it's that I got too much sleep last night," I said. "You're always complaining about being tired," was Mark's rather unsympathetic response. "No, I'm not!" I argued. Mark wisely didn't argue back, but our outing to the hardware store went downhill from there. I found myself impatient and irritable. The crowning blow came when a heavy piece of plywood fell on my foot. By the time we arrived home, I was in a foul mood.

It was not until later that I realized what went wrong. I had a sinful attitude. Instead of listening to Mark's observation and trying to learn from him, I got defensive. I didn't want to face the truth of his words. I went back to Mark and asked his forgiveness for being defensive and generally grouchy. Of course, he readily forgave me. It is hard to receive criticism graciously, isn't it? It is particularly difficult to face something ugly in ourselves that we have never before faced. We would much rather fool ourselves into thinking that we are perfect. Certainly we want others to think that about us! Perhaps that is how Peter felt in these verses.

Read—*Mark 14:27–31*

"You will all fall away," Jesus told them, "for it is written:
'I will strike the shepherd,
and the sheep will be scattered.'
But after I have risen, I will go ahead of you into Galilee."
Peter declared, "Even if all fall away, I will not."
"I tell you the truth," Jesus answered, "today—yes, tonight—before the rooster crows twice you yourself will disown me three times."
But Peter insisted emphatically, "Even if I have to die with you, I will never disown you." And all the others said the same.

Discuss

1. What did Jesus say to his disciples?
2. Peter didn't like what Jesus said. What did he say to Jesus?
3. Discuss what was right and what was wrong about Peter's attitude.
4. What did Jesus say that the disciples didn't seem to hear? Why not?

Final Thought

Twice Peter used the words "I will." Both times he was disagreeing with Jesus. We know that things turned out just as Jesus said they would. This is a warning for us. If God tells us something we don't want to hear, we still need to listen and accept it. Also we must recognize that we are weak. Like Peter, we can fall. Rather than boldly telling the Lord what "we will" do, we must ask him for strength to follow him.

Pray

Dear Lord, forgive us for arguing with you. Give us grace to accept your correction and strength to obey you.

Sing—*Alas! And Did My Savior Bleed*

Was it for sins that I had done
He groaned upon the tree?
Amazing pity, grace unknown,
And love beyond degree!

Do

Place the symbol of the shepherd's staff on your holiday tree.

Further Study for Adults

Read 1 Peter 5:1–9. What echoes do you find here of the incident recorded in Mark 14? What lessons has Peter learned by the time he writes this letter? In what practical ways can you humble yourself under God's mighty hand?

Do you ever have a hard time praying? I do. For me, prayer is the hardest part of obeying Christ. Every evening we pray with the kids before bed, and both kids have gone through stages when they did not want to pray. Once, when Laura was little, I said to her, "Laura, you don't need to say certain things. Just tell Jesus what you are feeling. He wants us to talk about everything with him—especially the things that are on our hearts." Laura loved to talk about her feelings, so suddenly she was willing to give prayer a go. "Lord," she prayed in a sweet, sincere voice, "I'm happy to tell you my feelings. And I'm happy for you to tell me your feelings. Please send me a message. Amen."

Jesus knew that there was nothing more important than communicating with the heavenly Father. There is much we cannot understand about how prayer works, but these things we do know. Jesus commanded us to pray. Jesus taught us how to pray. Jesus himself spent many, many hours alone with his Father in prayer.

I have to ask myself this question: if it was so important for Jesus to pray, when he is the sinless Son of God, isn't it even more necessary for me to pray?! I need God's forgiveness, mercy and help, his power and guidance, so much more desperately!

Read—*Luke 22:39–46*

Jesus went out as usual to the Mount of Olives, and his disciples followed him. On reaching the place, he said to them, "Pray that you will not fall into temptation." He withdrew about a stone's throw beyond them, knelt down and prayed, "Father, if you are willing, take this cup from me; yet not my will, but yours be done." An angel from heaven appeared to him and strengthened him. And being in anguish, he prayed more earnestly, and his sweat was like drops of blood falling to the ground.

When he rose from prayer and went back to the disciples, he found them asleep, exhausted from sorrow. "Why are you sleeping?" he asked them. "Get up and pray so that you will not fall into temptation."

Discuss
1. What did Jesus tell the disciples to do? Did they obey?
2. What were the words of Jesus' prayer? What do they mean?
3. Describe Jesus' prayer time. What do you suppose he felt?
4. How did God answer Jesus' prayer?

Final Thought
The disciples were tired and depressed. Passover had been unsettling, for Jesus had said many sad things. The last thing the disciples felt like doing was praying. They simply gave in to their feelings and went to sleep. Yet this night, of all nights, was the most crucial night for prayer. How like the disciples I am! Often I do what I feel like doing instead of the hard work of prayer.

Pray
Dear Lord, give me the strength of body, mind, and spirit to spend time in prayer with you. Help me, like Jesus, to offer myself to you and to be willing to accept your will, whatever it is.

Sing—*O Sacred Head, Now Wounded*

How art thou pale with anguish, With sore abuse and scorn;
How does that visage languish Which once was bright as morn!
Thy grief and bitter Passion Were all for sinners' gain;
Mine, mine was the transgression, But thine the deadly pain.

Do
Place the symbol of the disciples sleeping on your holiday tree.

Further Study for Adults
Read Revelation 5:8. Think about this picture of prayer. How can this help you better to pray?

FRIDAY

WEEK FOUR

Have you ever been betrayed? Someone whom you thought was your friend turned against you, trying to hurt you on purpose.

My friends Rich and Gina have been betrayed. They own a small business, and they hired Carol, a young woman who desperately needed a job. Carol had many needs, and Rich and Gina tried to help her in every way they could. They even allowed her to live in their home for three months until she could afford her own apartment. They treated her like a member of their own family. Carol seemed to blossom under their loving care.

Unfortunately, they discovered that Carol was not entirely honest. They spoke to her and gave her a second chance, then a third and a fourth. Finally, with regret, they had to let her go. The next thing they knew, Rich and Gina received a letter from a lawyer. Carol was taking them to court, declaring that they had done hurtful things to her—claims which were totally false.

Rich and Gina are baffled and hurt by Carol's actions. Jesus knows how it feels to be betrayed.

Read—*Luke 22:47–53*

While he was still speaking a crowd came up, and the man who was called Judas, one of the Twelve, was leading them. He approached Jesus to kiss him, but Jesus asked him, "Judas, are you betraying the Son of Man with a kiss?"

When Jesus' followers saw what was going to happen, they said, "Lord, should we strike with our swords?" And one of them struck the servant of the high priest, cutting off his right ear.

But Jesus answered, "No more of this!" And he touched the man's ear and healed him.

Then Jesus said to the chief priests, the officers of the temple guard, and the elders, who had come for him, "Am I leading a rebellion, that you have come with swords and clubs? Every day I was with you in the temple courts, and you did not lay a hand on me. But this is your hour—when darkness reigns."

Discuss

1. What was Judas doing in these verses?
2. Did Jesus become angry? What did he say?
3. What did Jesus' disciples do? Why?
4. How did Jesus respond to the disciples, to the servant, and to the Jewish leaders? What does that tell us about him?

Final Thought

Jesus met his enemies head-on. He gave himself over to them willingly, not out of weakness but out of his knowledge of God's purposes. His words to Judas and the leaders were clear and direct. They would be responsible for the evil choices they had made.

Pray

Dear Lord, let me never betray you. Give me the courage always to follow you and to love you.

Sing—*O Sacred Head, Now Wounded*

What language shall I borrow To thank thee, dearest friend,
For this thy dying sorrow, Thy pity without end?
Oh, make me thine forever, And, should I fainting be,
Lord, let me never, never Outlive my love to thee.

Do

Place the symbol of the lipstick print on your holiday tree.

Further Study for Adults

Read John 18:1–11. What additional details are included in John's account of this incident? Remember that John was actually there, whereas Luke interviewed eyewitnesses. What do Jesus' words and actions show us about his character?

SATURDAY

WEEK FOUR

Have you ever had to pick sides? "You can't be both our friend and her friend. Whose side are you on?" the group of popular girls says to you on the playground. Or, if you're a boy, you know that you might get beat up if you don't go along with a certain group of boys. You have a lot to lose—your popularity, or maybe your front teeth! Sometimes you turn your back on a friend and go along with the crowd because it seems like the safe thing to do at the time. You didn't plan to desert your friend. It's just that things happened so fast and you made the choice before you really thought about what you were doing.

Yesterday we read about Judas betraying Jesus. Judas planned this out and did it on purpose. Today we read about how Peter denied Jesus three times.

Read—*Luke 22:54–62*

Then seizing him, they led him away and took him into the house of the high priest. Peter followed at a distance. But when they had kindled a fire in the middle of the courtyard and had sat down together, Peter sat down with them. A servant girl saw him seated there in the firelight. She looked closely at him and said, "This man was with him."

But he denied it. "Woman, I don't know him," he said.

A little later someone else saw him and said, "You also are one of them."

"Man, I am not!" Peter replied.

About an hour later another asserted, "Certainly this fellow was with him, for he is a Galilean."

Peter replied, "Man, I don't know what you're talking about!" Just as he was speaking, the rooster crowed. The Lord turned and looked straight at Peter. Then Peter remembered the word the Lord had spoken to him: "Before the rooster crows today, you will disown me three times." And he went outside and wept bitterly.

Discuss
1. Did Peter mean to turn his back on Jesus? How do you know?
2. Why did Peter say that he didn't know Jesus?
3. What happened when the rooster crowed?
4. How did Peter feel after he realized what he had done?

Final Thought
In my mind's eye, I can see Jesus' face as he looked at Peter. His look was one of great sorrow. Jesus knew exactly what Peter said, just as he had predicted. That look must have gone straight through Peter's heart like a knife. How he must have wished that he could take back his words! Can you think of words that we say and things that we do which bring sorrow to Jesus?

Pray
Dear Lord Jesus, every time I sin against you, I deny you as Peter did. Keep me from sin, Lord.

Sing—*Alas! And Did My Savior Bleed*

But tears of grief cannot repay
The debt of love I owe;
Here, Lord, I give myself away:
It's all that I can do.

Do
Place the symbol of the rooster on your holiday tree.

Further Study for Adults
Read John 21:15–23. What parallels do you find between this passage and Peter's denial? What do you suppose was Jesus' purpose in this interaction? What does this show about Jesus' character? From what sins and failures has Jesus forgiven and restored you? How would Christ have you respond to his healing in your life?

Today is the Lord's Day, and once again we celebrate the risen Lord. The passage that follows is Part One of one of Jesus' appearances on the day that he was risen. Imagine yourself as one of these two disciples. What would you be feeling as you returned home from Passover in Jerusalem?

Read—*Luke 24:13–27*

Now that same day two of them were going to a village called Emmaus, about seven miles from Jerusalem. They were talking with each other about everything that had happened. As they talked and discussed these things with each other, Jesus himself came up and walked along with them; but they were kept from recognizing him.

He asked them, "What are you discussing together as you walk along?"

They stood still, their faces downcast. One of them, named Cleopas, asked him, "Are you only a visitor to Jerusalem and do not know the things that have happened there in these days?"

"What things?" he asked.

"About Jesus of Nazareth," they replied. "He was a prophet, powerful in word and deed before God and all the people. The chief priests and our rulers handed him over to be sentenced to death, and they crucified him; but we had hoped that he was the one who was going to redeem Israel. And what is more, it is the third day since all this took place. In addition, some of our women amazed us. They went to the tomb early this morning but didn't find his body. They came and told us that they had seen a vision of angels, who said he was alive. Then some of our companions went to the tomb and found it just as the women had said, but him they did not see."

He said to them, "How foolish you are, and how slow of heart to believe all that the prophets have spoken! Did not the Christ have to suffer these things and then enter his glory?" And beginning with Moses and all the Prophets, he explained to them what was said in all the Scriptures concerning himself.

Discuss

1. What was the mood of the disciples? Why?
2. What news did they tell Jesus?
3. How did Jesus respond? Why?
4. What did Jesus explain to them as they walked along?

Final Thought

I wish I had been there! Imagine taking a one-day seminar on the Old Testament, taught by the Lord himself! Whenever I study the Old Testament, I think of these verses. The entire Bible, from Genesis to Revelation, points to Jesus Christ and the salvation that he offers us by his death and resurrection. There are many things that I, like those two disciples, do not understand. I look forward to learning much more about God's ways when I get to heaven.

Pray

Dear Lord, thank you that from the very beginning of creation, it was your plan to come to earth to redeem us. We praise you.

Sing—*Christ the Lord Is Risen Today; Alleluia!*

Christ the Lord is ris'n today; Alleluia!
Christians, hasten on your way; Alleluia!
Offer praise with love replete, Alleluia!
At the paschal victim's feet. Alleluia!

Do

Place the symbol of the Bible on your holiday tree.

Further Study for Adults

Read Isaiah 53. Undoubtedly this was one of the scriptures that Jesus expounded to the disciples, as did Philip with the Ethiopian official in Acts 8. Summarize how this prophecy points to Jesus. What difference do these truths make in your life?

MONDAY

WEEK FIVE

Does anyone ever hurt your feelings or beat up on you? When I was a child, I didn't get beat up, but I was the brunt of quite a bit of teasing and insults. My family always praised, encouraged and supported me, but once I was outside my family circle, I was fair game for neighborhood kids and schoolmates.

My friend next door, Nancy, had an older brother, Todd, who delighted in tormenting me. I dreaded running into him, for I never knew what he would do to me next. Once Nancy and I were playing "fort" inside a sleeping bag, and Todd sat down on the opening of the sleeping bag, trapping us inside. I panicked, sure that we would suffocate. I do not know how long he trapped us in the sleeping bag, but it seemed like an eternity to me. Todd didn't mean to harm us. He was just being a typical brother, I suppose. But for me, it was a terrifying experience. To this day, I am afraid of small, confined places.

Jesus understands how we feel when we are insulted or abused. He experienced it himself.

Read—*Luke 22:63–71*

The men who were guarding Jesus began mocking and beating him. They blindfolded him and demanded, "Prophesy! Who hit you?" And they said many other insulting things to him.

At daybreak the council of the elders of the people, both the chief priests and teachers of the law, met together, and Jesus was led before them. "If you are the Christ," they said, "tell us."

Jesus answered, "If I tell you, you will not believe me, and if I asked you, you would not answer. But from now on, the Son of Man will be seated at the right hand of the mighty God."

They all asked, "Are you then the Son of God?"

He replied, "You are right in saying I am."

Then they said, "Why do we need any more testimony? We have heard it from his own lips."

Discuss

1. What did the guards do to Jesus?
2. Why do you think they did this?
3. What questions did the Jewish leaders ask Jesus?
4. How did Jesus answer them?

Final Thought

Jesus said nothing but the truth. Not only did he claim to be the very Son of God, but he told them that he would judge them from God's right hand. They should have trembled and begged for mercy. Instead they were insane with anger, intent only on killing him.

Pray

Dear Lord, you were insulted, abused, and not believed, and you suffered all this because of your love for me. Thank you for suffering and dying for me, so that I might have eternal life with you.

Sing—*When I Survey the Wondrous Cross*

See, from his head, his hands, his feet,
Sorrow and love flow mingled down.
Did e'er such love and sorrow meet,
Or thorns compose so rich a crown?

Do

Place the symbol of the whip on your holiday tree.

Further Study for Adults

Reflect again on Isaiah 53. How are these prophecies specifically fulfilled in the verses from Luke 22? See also Matthew 26:67,68 and 27:27–31.

TUESDAY

WEEK FIVE

Do you remember when we read that "Satan entered Judas" (Luke 22:3)? Judas decided to listen and obey Satan instead of Jesus. We don't know why Judas made that choice, but we have already seen what Satan led Judas to do. He betrayed Jesus for thirty pieces of silver. Today we will read about the final thing that Satan led Judas to do. It is a very sad story, but it is important for us to read. We need to remember Judas and how wrong choices lead to destruction. If we need a place to start, we can look at John 12:6, where we learn that Judas kept track of the money for the disciples and started to help himself to it. Sin usually begins with making wrong choices in small things. As you read, see where Judas' wrong choices led him.

Read—*Matthew 27:1–10*

Early in the morning, all the chief priests and the elders of the people came to the decision to put Jesus to death. They bound him, led him away and handed him over to Pilate, the governor.

When Judas, who had betrayed him, saw that Jesus was condemned, he was seized with remorse and returned the thirty silver coins to the chief priests and the elders. "I have sinned," he said, "for I have betrayed innocent blood."

"What is that to us?" they replied. "That's your responsibility."

So Judas threw the money into the temple and left. Then he went away and hanged himself.

The chief priests picked up the coins and said, "It is against the law to put this into the treasury, since it is blood money." So they decided to use the money to buy the potter's field as a burial place for foreigners. That is why it has been called the Field of Blood to this day. Then what was spoken by Jeremiah the prophet was fulfilled: "They took the thirty silver coins, the price set on him by the people of Israel, and they used them to buy the potter's field, as the Lord commanded me."

Discuss

1. How did Judas feel about what he had done?
2. What did he do about it?
3. What other choices could he have made?
4. What was the attitude of the chief priests?

Final Thought

If only Judas had gone to find Jesus and said to him, "I have sinned," the story would have turned out very differently. As it was, he went back to Satan, in the form of the chief priests. They couldn't care less that he was sorry for his sin. They had gotten what they wanted. Satan convinced Judas that there was no hope for him. Hopelessness and self-destruction come from Satan, not from the God of life and hope and forgiveness.

Pray

Dear Lord, keep me following you closely, so that I never choose the path of evil.

Sing—*My Faith Looks Up to Thee*

While life's dark maze I tread And griefs around me spread,
Be thou my guide:
Bid darkness turn to day, Wipe sorrow's tears away,
Nor let me ever stray From thee aside.

Do

Put the symbol of the coins on your holiday tree.

Further Study for Adults

Read 1 Peter 5:8–11. How is Satan depicted in these verses? How are we to resist him? What are specific areas of temptation in your life in which you especially need to be self-controlled and alert? Is there someone who can pray for you and hold you accountable in these areas? What promise does God give us in these verses?

WEDNESDAY

WEEK FIVE

Have you ever heard someone say, "That's a marriage made in heaven!"? Loving relationships are a gift from God. For many years I have prayed for good friendships for Mark and Laura. One year ago, I became aware of a new family at our church. They have two children, a boy Mark's age and a girl Laura's age. Since then, the kids have become the best of friends. These friendships have been a gift from God—they are friendships made in heaven.

The friendship in these verses was not made in heaven, however.

Read—Luke 23:1–12

Then the whole assembly rose and led him off to Pilate. And they began to accuse him, saying, "We have found this man subverting our nation. He opposes payment of taxes to Caesar and claims to be Christ, a king."

So Pilate asked Jesus, "Are you the king of the Jews?"

"Yes, it is as you say," Jesus replied.

Then Pilate announced to the chief priests and the crowd, "I find no basis for a charge against this man."

But they insisted, "He stirs up the people all over Judea by his teaching. He started in Galilee and has come all the way here."

On hearing this, Pilate asked if the man was a Galilean. When he learned that Jesus was under Herod's jurisdiction, he sent him to Herod, who was also in Jerusalem at that time.

When Herod saw Jesus, he was greatly pleased, because for a long time he had been wanting to see him. From what he had heard about him, he hoped to see him perform some miracle. He plied him with many questions, but Jesus gave him no answer. The chief priests and the teachers of the law were standing there, vehemently accusing him. Then Herod and his soldiers ridiculed and mocked him. Dressing him in an elegant robe, they sent him back to Pilate. That day Herod and Pilate became friends—before this they had been enemies.

Discuss
1. What lies did the people tell about Jesus?
2. Why did Pilate send Jesus to Herod?
3. Why was Herod happy to see Jesus?
4. Why did Herod and Pilate become friends on that day?

Final Thought
Pilate and Herod became friends that day because they became partners in crime. They were both responsible for Jesus' death. Pilate knew in his heart that Jesus did not deserve death, but he buckled under the pressure of the people. In these verses, he tried to wiggle out of his responsibility. Herod just wanted a good show. When Jesus refused to entertain him, Herod put on a show of his own. God will not satisfy our idle curiosity. Nor will he let us wiggle out of our responsibility.

Pray
Dear Lord, help us not to be like Herod or Pilate. Help us to honor you as God and to obey you responsibly.

Sing—*O Sacred Head, Now Wounded*

How art thou pale with anguish, With sore abuse and scorn;
How does that visage languish Which once was bright as morn!
Thy grief and bitter Passion Were all for sinners' gain;
Mine, mine was the transgression, But thine the deadly pain.

Do
Place the symbol of the crown on your holiday tree.

Further Study for Adults
Compare and contrast Jesus' responses to Pilate and Herod. Why do you think he responded the way he did in each of these situations? Read Isaiah 53:7. Does this lend any further insight into Jesus' actions? What character qualities did Jesus exhibit? How can you grow in these areas?

THURSDAY

WEEK FIVE

I am ashamed to admit that I am a big chicken. I want to be liked, and sometimes I do wrong things to make others like me. For instance, take complaining. I know that complaining is a sin. When I complain, I am really saying, "I don't like what you are doing in my life, Lord. Either you can't control it or you don't care about me." I know very well that God loves me and he is in charge of my life. So why do I complain? Besides it being a sinful habit, complaining sometimes helps me fit in with others. Everyone likes to complain. If others are complaining, it is easier to go along with it. I am just beginning to learn to say, "Stop! This is not helpful. Let's be thankful for our blessings instead." But that takes courage.

Read—*Luke 23:13–25*

Pilate called together the chief priests, the rulers and the people, and said to them, "You brought me this man as one who was inciting the people to rebellion. I have examined him in your presence and have found no basis for your charges against him. Neither has Herod, for he sent him back to us; as you can see, he has done nothing to deserve death. Therefore, I will punish him and then release him."

With one voice they cried out, "Away with this man! Release Barabbas to us!" (Barabbas had been thrown into prison for an insurrection in the city, and for murder.)

Wanting to release Jesus, Pilate appealed to them again. But they kept shouting, "Crucify him! Crucify him!"

For the third time he spoke to them: "Why? What crime has this man committed? I have found in him no grounds for the death penalty. Therefore I will have him punished and then release him."

But with loud shouts they insistently demanded that he be crucified, and their shouts prevailed. So Pilate decided to grant their demand. He released the man who had been thrown into prison for insurrection and murder, the one they asked for, and surrendered Jesus to their will.

Discuss

1. What did Pilate say about Jesus?
2. Pilate thought of a way he could get out of killing Jesus. He would give them a choice. What choice did Pilate offer?
3. What was Barabbas like? Why did they choose to kill Jesus?
4. Why did Pilate finally decide to crucify Jesus?

Final Thought

Pilate believed that Jesus was innocent. He wanted to release him. Why then did he give in to the crowd's angry demands? He was afraid. He did not have the courage to stand up for the truth. Would you have done differently? If we want to have courage when the big tests come, we need to develop courage in the little things. Today, remember to tell the truth when it might get you in trouble. Develop courage muscles!

Pray

Dear Lord, help me to have courage today to stand up for the truth and to stand up for you.

Sing—*My Song Is Love Unknown*

They rise, and needs will have My dear Lord made away;
A murderer they save, The prince of life they slay.
Yet cheerful he to suff'ring goes,
That he his foes from thence might free.

Do

Place the symbol of the hammer on your holiday tree. A hammer represents judgment.

Further Study for Adults

Read 2 Corinthians 5:21, Hebrews 4:15, 1 Peter 2:22, 1 John 3:5. What do these verses tell us about Jesus? Compare these with Pilate's words. In order for Jesus' sacrifice to fulfill the law's demands, he needed to be the Lamb without blemish. Write a psalm of thanks to the Lamb.

FRIDAY

WEEK FIVE

Children can be so cruel to one another. When I was in junior high school, I was not a part of the "in" crowd. I wore braces and glasses and had pimples on my face. I didn't swear or dance. I studied hard and got good grades, so I had the reputation of being a "brain." The boys did not flock to me. Rather, they made fun of me. They called me names and played mean tricks on me. The popular girls didn't call me names to my face, but I knew they said bad things about me behind my back. They just gave me looks that said, "You are SO weird!"

Looking back on that time, I realize that in part I deserved the reputation I had. While other kids were rebelling against their parents, I rebelled against the popular crowd by being especially weird on purpose. But partly, I was rejected for being an outspoken Christian. I started an after school "Discussion Club" to discuss the Bible and issues like evolution. I stood up for the underdogs, like my friend Mary. And my lifestyle was different than that of the popular kids.

Often people make fun of those who are different than they are. Sometimes they abuse and kill them. Many people have suffered terribly simply because they are a different race than the majority. The handicapped have often been abused. Jesus too was different. He was Jewish (so he was different than the Romans) and he was holy, so he was different than all of us.

Read—Mark 15:16–20

The soldiers led Jesus away into the palace (that is, the Praetorium) and called together the whole company of soldiers. They put a purple robe on him, then twisted together a crown of thorns and set it on him. And they began to call out to him, "Hail, king of the Jews!" Again and again they struck him on the head with a staff and spit on him. Falling on their knees, they paid homage to him. And when they had mocked him, they took off the purple robe and put his own clothes on him. Then they led him out to crucify him.

Discuss

1. How did the soldiers dress up Jesus?
2. What did they yell and what did they do to him?
3. Why do you think they did this?
4. Jesus said that his followers should be ready to be treated the same way. Are you ready for this? What can you do to prepare?

Final Thought

Little did the soldiers know that in reality Jesus is the creator of the world and ruler over all things. He sits on the throne in heaven and one day will judge every person. Yet he allowed himself to be treated this way. Why? That is the mystery of his great love for us. He suffered for us, so that we might be forgiven and live a wonderful life of knowing him, now and forever.

Pray

Dear Lord, thank you so much for suffering as you did for my sake. I accept your gift of forgiveness and love.

Sing—*O Sacred Head, Now Wounded*

O sacred head, now wounded, With grief and shame weighed down,
Now scornfully surrounded With thorns, thine only crown;
O sacred head, what glory, What bliss till now was thine!
Yet, though despised and gory, I joy to call thee mine.

Do

Place the symbol of the crown of thorns on your holiday tree.

Further Study for Adults

Read Hebrews 1:1–4. Here is a glimpse of Christ's glory. Write in your own words all that this passage tells about Jesus. The fact that Jesus "sat down at the right hand" of God means that his redemptive work is complete, and he is now ruling as Lord over all things. Write a hymn of praise to Christ.

SATURDAY

WEEK FIVE

The year 1992 was a difficult, dark year for me. I suffered some disappointments which caused me to question my abilities and my direction in life. These brought up other disappointments from my past. I began to relive old hurts that had been buried for years. I realize now that I was depressed. There was so much hurt in my heart that I longed to be in heaven.

That is very selfish. I was mired in self-centeredness. Actually, my disappointments were so tiny compared to the hurts of many other people in this sinful, hurting world.

If anyone ever had reason to be depressed, it was Jesus. He had done no wrong. He had given everything he had to help others. And what did he get in return? Rejection. Abuse. Mockery. Death.

Read—*Luke 23:26–34*

As they led him away, they seized Simon from Cyrene, who was on his way in from the country, and put the cross on him and made him carry it behind Jesus. A large number of people followed him, including women who mourned and wailed for him. Jesus turned and said to them, "Daughters of Jerusalem, do not weep for me; weep for yourselves and for your children. For the time will come when you will say, 'Blessed are the barren women, the wombs that never bore and the breasts that never nursed!' Then

"'they will say to the mountains, "Fall on us!"
and to the hills, "Cover us!"'

For if men do these things when the tree is green, what will happen when it is dry?"

Two other men, both criminals, were also led out with him to be executed. When they came to the place called the Skull, there they crucified him, along with the criminals—one on his right, the other on his left. Jesus said, "Father, forgive them, for they do not know what they are doing." And they divided up his clothes by casting lots.

Discuss
1. Name all the characters that come into this passage.
2. What part did each person play?
3. What did Jesus say to the women who were following behind him, weeping? Why did he say this?
4. What did Jesus pray for as he was being crucified? Would you have prayed for this? Why or why not?

Final Thought
Jesus' words show that he gave no thought to himself—his concern, even at this horrible moment, was all for others. I would have wanted the women to weep for me. I would have prayed that God would help me, deliver me, ease my pain. Not so with Jesus. He was concerned that Jerusalem repent before disaster befell them. And he was concerned that his killers be forgiven by God. In words and actions, Jesus was totally selfless.

Pray
Dear Lord, make me like Jesus. Let me be more concerned for others than I am for myself.

Sing—*O Sacred Head, Now Wounded*

How art thou pale with anguish, With sore abuse and scorn;
How does that visage languish Which once was bright as morn!
Thy grief and bitter Passion Were all for sinners' gain;
Mine, mine was the transgression, But thine the deadly pain.

Do
Place the symbol of the three crosses on your holiday tree.

Further Study for Adults
Read Matthew 5:43–48 and 6:14–15. How did Jesus exemplify these principals? Reflect on your relationships, both current and past. Is there any injury or disappointment which you have not forgiven? What steps can you take today to begin the process of forgiveness and healing?

SUNDAY

FIFTH SUNDAY IN LENT

My two sisters Elaine and Carolyn are two of my best friends on earth. We are not able to see each other nearly as often as we would like, for I live in Virginia, Elaine in Minnesota, and Carolyn in Montana. The last time we were together was two years ago. We had one wonderful opportunity to be alone together, just the three Martin sisters. We went out to lunch at a Chinese restaurant near Elaine's home. For several hours we sat talking, laughing, and thoroughly enjoying one another. We were able to share our hearts, knowing that the other two sisters understood us and loved us completely—just as we are. Suddenly I realized what a taste of heaven this was. "You guys," I said (we say that even to girls and women in Minnesota), "it doesn't get any better than this!"

We read today about another wonderful time of fellowship as we pick up where last Sunday's reading ended. Remember how Jesus appeared to the two disciples on the road to Emmaus? Briefly retell the story, keeping in mind that this happened on the day of Jesus' resurrection.

Read—Luke 24:28–35

As they approached the village to which they were going, Jesus acted as if he were going farther. But they urged him strongly, "Stay with us, for it is nearly evening; the day is almost over." So he went in to stay with them.

When he was at the table with them, he took bread, gave thanks, broke it and began to give it to them. Then their eyes were opened and they recognized him, and he disappeared from their sight. They asked each other, "Were not our hearts burning within us while he talked with us on the road and opened the Scriptures to us?"

They got up and returned at once to Jerusalem. There they found the Eleven and those with them, assembled together and saying, "It is true! The Lord has risen and has appeared to Simon." Then the two told what had happened on the way, and how Jesus was recognized by them when he broke the bread.

Discuss

1. When the disciples got to their village, what did they say to Jesus? Why do you think they wanted him to stay?
2. When did they recognize Jesus?
3. What did they say to each other when Jesus disappeared?
4. What did they do then? Why do you suppose they went back to Jerusalem?

Final Thought

Even before the two disciples knew it was Jesus, they knew that they did not want to part with this stranger. As Jesus walked and talked with them, teaching them, their "hearts burned within" them—burned with excitement and joy. If we love the Lord, we will someday be with him in person in heaven. And our hearts will burn as they have never burned before—with joy. Even now we can experience this as we come to know him more deeply.

Pray

Dear Lord, I want to know you. Help me to walk with you and learn of you, even as these disciples did.

Sing—*The King of Love My Shepherd Is*

The King of love my shepherd is,
Whose goodness faileth never;
I nothing lack if I am his
And he is mine forever.

Do

Place the symbol of a pair of glasses on your holiday tree.

Further Study for Adults

Read John 17:1–5. This is the "High Priestly Prayer" of Jesus, the prayer he prayed for himself, for his disciples, and for us, on the night he was betrayed. Write down the truths these verses teach about the Father, about the Son, and about us. How does Jesus define eternal life?

MONDAY

WEEK SIX

Have you ever disobeyed a rule or broken a law? What are some examples of rules you have broken? What was the punishment? Every single person except for Jesus has broken laws, for unlike Jesus we are all sinners. Take the speed limit, for example. In my town, the speed limit is twenty-five miles an hour. I try to obey that law, but sometimes I am not paying attention and I find myself zooming along at thirty-five or forty miles an hour. So far I have never gotten a ticket for speeding. If someday I do, I will not be happy about it, but I will accept it. I know that countless times I have deserved speeding tickets and not gotten them.

In today's reading, three men were being punished. Two deserved punishment, one did not. And the punishment that all three were getting was the harshest punishment of all—death on a cross.

Read—*Luke 23:35–43*

The people stood watching, and the rulers even sneered at him. They said, "He saved others; let him save himself if he is the Christ of God, the Chosen One."

The soldiers also came up and mocked him. They offered him wine vinegar and said, "If you are the king of the Jews, save yourself."

There was a written notice above him, which read: THIS IS THE KING OF THE JEWS.

One of the criminals who hung there hurled insults at him: "Aren't you the Christ? Save yourself and us!"

But the other criminal rebuked him. "Don't you fear God," he said, "since you are under the same sentence? We are punished justly, for we are getting what our deeds deserve. But this man has done nothing wrong."

Then he said, "Jesus, remember me when you come into your kingdom."

Jesus answered him, "I tell you the truth, today you will be with me in paradise."

Discuss

1. Who mocked Jesus? What did they say?
2. How did Jesus respond?
3. What did the second criminal understand about himself? What did he understand about Jesus? What did he ask of Jesus?
4. What did Jesus promise this criminal?

Final Thought

This criminal understood what even Jesus' disciples did not yet understand. He knew that he was a sinner and deserved death. He also knew that Jesus had done nothing wrong. But most amazing, he understood that Jesus' kingdom was not an earthly kingdom. As others sneered at a broken, dying man, the criminal humbly asked a favor of Jesus as King. Jesus had no words for the mockers, but for the man of faith, criminal though he was, Jesus, King of kings, gave assurance of eternal life.

Pray

Dearest Lord Jesus, even though you were the King of heaven, you died a sinner's death for me. I thank you.

Sing—*Alas! And Did My Savior Bleed*

Alas! And did my Savior bleed, And did my sov'reign die?
Would he devote that sacred head For sinners such as I?

Was it for sins that I had done He groaned upon the tree?
Amazing pity, grace unknown, And love beyond degree!

Do

Place the symbol of the sign reading "THE KING OF THE JEWS" on your holiday tree.

Further Study for Adults

Read Psalm 22:1, 15–18. How did David's words of distress prove prophetic? See also John 19:23–24. In both Matthew's and Mark's accounts, Jesus quoted Psalm 22:1 from the cross. See Matthew 27:46 and Mark 15:34. What did Jesus mean by this?

TUESDAY

WEEK SIX

Two years ago I learned that a single friend on staff at the church, Martha, would soon be needing a new living situation. She was renting a house with two other women, but the owners had decided to sell the house. Martha could not afford to rent her own apartment because of the high cost of living in our area. Several of her previous roommate situations had left deep wounds, and Martha was afraid to start over again with another group.

I mentioned Martha's predicament to Jim, and we decided to offer her a room in our home. We thought that we could provide a stable, loving family environment for Martha. And she would provide another adult role model for our children, for Martha is a very committed Christian.

Now, two years later, Martha is still with us. As prepared as we thought we were, there have been many surprises. Martha had no idea when she came to live here that at the Hibbard house, Saturday mornings sometimes start at 6:30 with the banging of hammers and the screeching of saws. (The next time she interviews a prospective roommate or housemate, she will be sure to ask about home improvement projects!)

The biggest surprise for me has been all that I have learned. God has used Martha to teach me about communicating more honestly and directly with family and friends, especially when difficulties arise.

We have become family to each other in a special way. It is the love of Jesus Christ that brought us together and keeps us together. We read of just such a bond in today's passage.

Read—John 19:25–27

Near the cross of Jesus stood his mother, his mother's sister, Mary the wife of Clopas, and Mary Magdalene. When Jesus saw his mother there, and the disciple whom he loved standing nearby, he said to his mother, "Dear woman, here is your son," and to the disciple, "Here is your mother." From that time on, this disciple took her into his home.

Discuss

1. Who was standing near the cross?
2. What did Jesus call his mother?
3. Why do you think Jesus gave his mother and John to each other?
4. What does it say about the three Marys and John, that they were standing near the cross? Where were Jesus' other followers?

Final Thought

Jesus looked down from the cross and saw the two people on earth who loved him most. He knew they would miss him terribly. He provided for their needs by allowing them to care for each other. Even today, Jesus makes the same arrangement. If we love Jesus, we are given the responsibility of loving and taking care of other believers as if they were our own family—for in Christ, we are family.

Pray

Dear Lord, thank you that we belong to your family. Help us to care for our brothers and sisters in Christ.

Sing—*When I Survey the Wondrous Cross*

See, from his head, his hands, his feet,
Sorrow and love flow mingled down.
Did e'er such love and sorrow meet,
Or thorns compose so rich a crown?

Do

Place the symbol of the heart on your holiday tree.

Further Study for Adults

Read 1 John 3:16–18. These verses are penned by John, who also wrote the above account. And he was the one referred to as "the disciple whom he (Jesus) loved." What insights into John's character can we glean from both these passages? What is the message for us today?

WEDNESDAY

WEEK SIX

How do you feel if you have had a fight with your parents or your best friend? When something comes between someone I love and me, I am utterly miserable. Laura is like me in this regard. Usually we are the closest of friends, but we also have some real knock-down, drag-out fights (verbal fights, that is). Often they have to do with cleaning her room, which is not one of Laura's favorite activities. After a tiff, Laura stays in her room for a while. But before long, she seeks me out with a sincere apology. She cannot bear to let anything stand between us.

Even though Jesus never did anything wrong, something came between him and his father. Can you guess what it was? It was our sin. Jesus carried our sin on the cross. Because of our sin, the heavenly Father had to turn his face from his Son.

Read—*Matthew 27:45–54*

From the sixth hour until the ninth hour darkness came over all the land. About the ninth hour Jesus cried out in a loud voice, "*Eloi, Eloi, lama sabach-thani?*"—which means, "My God, my God, why have you forsaken me?"

When some of those standing there heard this, they said, "He's calling Elijah."

Immediately one of them ran and got a sponge. He filled it with wine vinegar, put it on a stick, and offered it to Jesus to drink. The rest said, "Now leave him alone. Let's see if Elijah comes to save him."

And when Jesus had cried out again in a loud voice, he gave up his spirit.

At that moment the curtain of the temple was torn in two from top to bottom. The earth shook and the rocks split. The tombs broke open and the bodies of many holy people who had died were raised to life. They came out of the tombs, and after Jesus' resurrection they went into the holy city and appeared to many people.

When the centurion and those with him who were guarding Jesus saw the earthquake and all that had happened, they were terrified, and exclaimed, "Surely he was the Son of God!"

Discuss
1. The sixth hour was noon. What time was it when Jesus died?
2. What did he cry out? What did others think he said?
3. What unusual things happened when Jesus died?
4. How did people react? What did they feel, do, say?

Final Thought
The most painful part of the crucifixion for Jesus was not the nails in his hands and feet. It was the pain of separation from his Father. At that moment he felt the guilt and misery from the sin of the whole world. If we have ever felt totally alone and abandoned, we have a tiny glimmer of the loneliness of Jesus on the cross. Jesus experienced this so that we would not have to be separated from God in eternity.

Pray
Dear Lord, thank you for suffering for our sins so that we can live with you in joy and bliss forever.

Sing—*Alas! And Did My Savior Bleed*

Well might the sun in darkness hide And shut its glories in
When God, the mighty maker, died For his own creatures' sin.

Thus might I hide my blushing face While his dear cross appears,
Dissolve my heart in thankfulness, And melt away my tears.

Do
Place the symbol of a sponge on your holiday tree.

Further Study for Adults
Reflect on the unusual supernatural occurrences which accompanied Jesus' death. Why do you think these things happened? Can you speculate on a possible significance for each occurrence? What conclusion did the centurion reach? Even with all these miraculous events, we do not know of anyone else who reached the same conclusion. Apparently the centurion's heart was open to truth. Are we open to God's truth?

THURSDAY

WEEK SIX

Have you ever seen the sky grow black in the middle of the day? I remember watching a storm move in from the Northeast one day when our family was vacationing at the ocean. We were staying at a cottage on the Outer Banks of North Carolina, barrier islands on the Atlantic coast. We stood on the balcony where we could see the gray line where ocean meets sky. First we saw a dark slice of sky to the left, which is the direction of Northeast from which the most violent storms come. Sailors call them "nor'easters." Slowly the dark bank of storm clouds moved toward us, their edge as sharp and straight as a knife. The rest of the sky was blue, with high, fluffy clouds. A thrill of excitement and fear shot through us. Below the dark portion of sky, we could no longer see the horizon. It was like a black curtain moving toward us. When it was almost upon us, the wind hit like a freight train. The cottage, which was up on stilts, creaked and swayed. We ran inside as the rain began to pelt down. In half an hour, the day at the beach went from being sunny and pleasant to being dark, foreboding, and violent.

Read—*Luke 23:44–49*

It was now about the sixth hour, and darkness came over the whole land until the ninth hour, for the sun stopped shining. And the curtain of the temple was torn in two. Jesus called out with a loud voice, "Father, into your hands I commit my spirit." When he had said this, he breathed his last.

The centurion, seeing what had happened, praised God and said, "Surely this was a righteous man." When all the people who had gathered to witness this sight saw what took place, they beat their breasts and went away. But all those who knew him, including the women who had followed him from Galilee, stood at a distance, watching these things.

Discuss

1. How is this account of Jesus' death similar to the account that we read yesterday from Matthew?
2. What are the differences?
3. What did Jesus cry out as he died? What does this mean?
4. How did the various people watching react to these things?

Final Thought

The temple curtain separated the Holy Place from the Most Holy Place (or the Holiest of Holies). This was a place that no one was allowed to go, for God's presence was there in a special way. Only the high priest could go there once a year, on the Day of Atonement, to pray for the sins of the people. When the curtain tore in two from top to bottom, it was God's way of saying that Jesus' death made a way for us to come directly to God. No more do we need priests and sacrifices.

Pray

Dear Lord, thank you for making a way for us to come to God.

Sing—*Alas! And Did My Savior Bleed*

Well might the sun in darkness hide And shut its glories in
When God, the mighty maker, died For his own creatures' sin.

Thus might I hide my blushing face While his dear cross appears,
Dissolve my heart in thankfulness, And melt away my tears.

Do

Place the symbol of curtain fabric on your holiday tree.

Further Study for Adults

Read Hebrews 10:19–23. What insights do these verses give us concerning the significance of the torn temple curtain? To what is the curtain compared? What commands are given here? How does knowledge of Christ's high priestly work help us to follow these commands? Like the curtain, Jesus' body was torn to open the way to God. How do we avail ourselves of his presence?

FRIDAY

WEEK SIX

Each year before Memorial Day, my mother travels to her home town of Cokato, Minnesota to plant flowers on her parents' graves. I remember the cemetery as a lovely and fairly interesting spot on a grassy hill with big, gnarled old oak trees on the crest. My sister and I wandered around admiring all the tall and stately granite markers. Our grandparents' markers were the humblest variety, simply set in the ground. After Mom planted the red geraniums, she walked around the cemetery to see who had died that year.

As a teenager, I came up with philosophical reasons against this ritual. I argued that Grandma and Grandpa were in heaven. Surely they didn't care about flowers on their graves. But Mom stood firm. "This is the one thing I do each year to honor my parents," she replied. "When other families go out to the cemetery, they see that Carl and Hilma Ring have been remembered and honored." As I have grown up, I have changed my mind. What do you think? Read about how one man helped and honored Jesus after Jesus' death.

Read—*Luke 23:50–56*

Now there was a man named Joseph, a member of the Council, a good and upright man, who had not consented to their decision and action. He came from the Judean town of Arimathea and he was waiting for the kingdom of God. Going to Pilate, he asked for Jesus' body. Then he took it down, wrapped it in linen cloth and placed it in a tomb cut in the rock, one in which no one had yet been laid. It was Preparation Day, and the Sabbath was about to begin.

The women who had come with Jesus from Galilee followed Joseph and saw the tomb and how his body was laid in it. Then they went home and prepared spices and perfumes. But they rested on the Sabbath in obedience to the commandment.

Discuss

1. This Joseph was not the same Joseph as Jesus' earthly father. (Mary's husband apparently died before Jesus started his ministry.) What do we learn about this Joseph?
2. What did Joseph ask of Pilate?
3. What did he do to Jesus' body? Why?
4. What did the women do? Why?

Final Thought

We find in Joseph a man of courage. He stood up for Jesus when everyone else on the Council wanted to have Jesus killed. (He probably was not there when the Sanhedrin met that night and decided to bring Jesus before Pilate to have him sentenced to death.) Since he could not prevent Jesus' death, he did what he could do. He asked Pilate for Jesus' body (another courageous move) and provided for Jesus' burial.

Pray

Dear Lord, help me to be courageous like Joseph. And show me the good I can do out of devotion to you.

Sing—*My Song Is Love Unknown*

In life, no house, no home My Lord on earth might have;
In death, no friendly tomb But what a stranger gave.
What may I say? Heav'n was his home;
But mine the tomb wherein he lay.

Do

Place the symbol of the strip of linen on your holiday tree.

Further Study for Adults

Read Isaiah 53:9. How was Jesus' burial a fulfillment of this prophecy? Reflect also on the words to the above hymn. How is Jesus' tomb our home? What new home did Christ's death secure for us? Read Hebrews 11:8–10, 13–16, and Jesus' promise in John 14:1–4. How does this hope influence your life?

SATURDAY

WEEK SIX

This morning our phone rang at 5:45. It was a police officer. He said that they had caught two youths with bikes that they thought belonged to us, stolen out of our shed. We quickly dressed and met the police outside. The bikes were in the trunk of one of the cars. One belonged to Mark, the other to Martha. Apparently, the two young men, one seventeen and one eighteen, had been seen in our neighborhood trying to break into a car. The police were on their way to investigate when this officer spotted the two of them on the bike path with the two bikes. Martha's bike had a locked chain threaded through the back wheel and the frame, so they couldn't just take off. They were trying to get the chain off when the police caught them.

Martha's safety precautions saved the day. Because of the lock on her bike, the young men were caught and our bikes were returned. When we put the bikes back in the shed, we put a combination lock on our shed door.

Today's reading has to do with security measures which were taken with Jesus' body after he died.

Read—*Matthew 27:62–66*

The next day, the one after Preparation Day, the chief priests and the Pharisees went to Pilate. "Sir," they said, "we remember that while he was still alive that deceiver said, 'After three days I will rise again.' So give the order for the tomb to be made secure until the third day. Otherwise, his disciples may come and steal the body and tell the people that he has been raised from the dead. This last deception will be worse than the first."

"Take a guard," Pilate answered. "Go, make the tomb as secure as you know how." So they went and made the tomb secure by putting a seal on the stone and posting the guard.

Discuss

1. Who was worried about Jesus' body being stolen?
2. Why were they concerned about this?
3. How would a report that Jesus was raised from the dead be worse for the Jewish leaders than the things Jesus said and did before his crucifixion?
4. How did Pilate respond to their request?

Final Thought

Even these fearful actions taken by Jesus' enemies were a part of God's wonderful plan. The sealed tomb and the Roman guard are evidence that when the tomb was found empty, it was not because the disciples stole the body. We learn in the next chapter that the guards saw the angel who rolled away the stone. The guards fainted, then later reported to the chief priests, and accepted a bribe to lie about what happened.

Pray

Dear Lord, how wonderful you are. Even the evil of men works out for your good purposes.

Sing—*Rock of Ages, Cleft for Me*

Rock of Ages, cleft for me, Let me hide myself in thee;
Let the water and the blood, From thy riven side which flowed,
Be of sin the double cure: Cleanse me from its guilt and pow'r.

Do

Place the symbol of the lock on your holiday tree.

Further Study for Adults

Read about the guards in Matthew 28:4, 11–15. How do you suppose Matthew knew about this? I suspect that either one of the guards later became a Christian and told the disciples the truth, or else it was a chief priest or one of their servants. How did the chief priests' sin snowball? What does that teach us about the effect of sin?

Today we celebrate Palm Sunday, the day Jesus rode into Jerusalem on the colt to the cheers of the excited throng. We read about it earlier during week two of Lent. Last time we read the verses from Luke; this time we look at the account from the Gospel of Mark. Did you go to church this morning? What special things did you do there to celebrate Jesus' triumphal entry?

Read—*Mark 11:1–11*

As they approached Jerusalem and came to Bethphage and Bethany at the Mount of Olives, Jesus sent two of his disciples, saying to them, "Go to the village ahead of you, and just as you enter it, you will find a colt tied there, which no one has ever ridden. Untie it and bring it here. If anyone asks you, 'Why are you doing this?' tell him, 'The Lord needs it and will send it back here shortly.'"

They went and found a colt outside in the street, tied at a doorway. As they untied it, some people standing there asked, "What are you doing, untying that colt?" They answered as Jesus had told them to, and the people let them go. When they brought the colt to Jesus and threw their cloaks over it, he sat on it. Many people spread their cloaks on the road, while others spread branches they had cut in the fields. Those who went ahead and those who followed shouted,

"Hosanna!"
"Blessed is he who comes in the name of the Lord!"
"Blessed is the coming kingdom of our father David!"
"Hosanna in the highest!"

Jesus entered Jerusalem and went to the temple. He looked around at everything, but since it was already late, he went out to Bethany with the Twelve.

Discuss

1. Read Zechariah 9:9. Who does the prophet say would come riding into Jerusalem on a donkey?
2. What was Jesus saying to the Jewish leaders when he rode into Jerusalem on a colt?
3. Did the people know this? How can you tell?
4. What did the people do and say to honor Jesus?

Final Thought

Jesus declared himself Messiah that day by riding on the colt into Jerusalem just as the prophet said. The people knew it, for they blessed the kingdom of David, which was to be the kingdom of the Messiah. Jesus knew that this would be the last straw for the Jewish leaders, that after this, they would find a way to arrest and kill him. Jesus brought this about on purpose, for he knew he had to die for our sins and be raised.

Pray

Thank you, Lord Jesus, for coming to Jerusalem to suffer and die for me. I bless you as King of kings forever.

Sing—*My Song Is Love Unknown*

Sometimes they strew his way And his sweet praises sing;
Resounding all the day Hosannas to their King.
Then "Crucify!" is all their breath,
And for his death they thirst and cry.

Do

Place the symbol of the palm branches on your holiday tree.

Further Study for Adults

Read John 12:12–19. What additional insights does the disciple John give us in his account? What were the reasons for the big crowd? How did the Pharisees react? Contrast Jesus' point of view with that of the disciples, the crowd, and the Pharisees.

MONDAY

HOLY WEEK

When you hear the word "substitute," what do you think of? If you go to school, you probably think of a substitute teacher. That is a teacher other than your regular one, who comes in to teach when your teacher cannot come to school. Or if you are a sports fan, you think of a player who fills in for another player in case of injury or penalty. In both cases, one person takes another person's place. This week as we prepare to celebrate Jesus' death and resurrection, we will be thinking about some of the different ways in which these events are important to us. One way in which Jesus' death is important is that he was our substitute.

Read—*Luke 23:13–25*

Pilate called together the chief priests, the rulers and the people, and said to them, "You brought me this man as one who was inciting the people to rebellion. I have examined him in your presence and have found no basis for your charges against him. Neither has Herod, for he sent him back to us; as you can see, he has done nothing to deserve death. Therefore, I will punish him and then release him."

With one voice they cried out, "Away with this man! Release Barabbas to us!" (Barabbas had been thrown into prison for an insurrection in the city, and for murder.)

Wanting to release Jesus, Pilate appealed to them again. But they kept shouting, "Crucify him! Crucify him!"

For the third time he spoke to them: "Why? What crime has this man committed? I have found in him no grounds for the death penalty. Therefore I will have him punished and then release him."

But with loud shouts they insistently demanded that he be crucified, and their shouts prevailed. So Pilate decided to grant their demand. He released the man who had been thrown into prison for insurrection and murder, the one they asked for, and surrendered Jesus to their will.

Discuss

1. Who deserved to be punished? What had he done?
2. Who took the punishment? What had Jesus done wrong?
3. How was Jesus a substitute for Barabbas?
4. If you were Barabbas, how would you feel when you learned that you were free and that Jesus had died in your place?

Final Thought

We are no different than Barabbas. We have all done wrong things and deserve to be punished. If we have broken God's law (which we have), the punishment for that is death. Jesus was our substitute, just as he was Barabbas' substitute. He took the death penalty in our place. Because of his death, those who trust in him are pardoned and free!

Pray

Dear Lord Jesus, thank you for being my substitute. I trust in you for my salvation.

Sing—*O Sacred Head, Now Wounded*

How art thou pale with anguish, With sore abuse and scorn;
How does that visage languish Which once was bright as morn!
Thy grief and bitter Passion Were all for sinners' gain;
Mine, mine was the transgression, But thine the deadly pain.

Do

Place the symbol of the ball and chain on your holiday tree.

Further Study for Adults

What does Isaiah 53 teach about the substitutionary death of Christ? The Book of Common Prayer refers to "remission of our sins, and all other benefits of his passion." What are some of the benefits of Christ's passion (his suffering and death) according to Isaiah 53?

From the day that Laura could wriggle in and out of her clothes, she has been a clothes-changer. This happened at a very early age, probably one and a half or two, and at age eleven, she has not changed a bit in this regard. I used to tear my hair out when I would go into her room and find the floor littered with articles of clothing—all of which she had worn for a portion of the day. Sometimes she went through ten outfits in a single day! Things have improved since Laura started doing her own laundry. Reducing her wardrobe also helped. Sometimes when Laura has a friend over, she and her friend switch clothes, just for fun. Have you ever done this?

Remember that yesterday we thought about how Jesus was our substitute? Another way to say it is that Jesus traded places with us. Or that he switched clothes with us.

Have you ever seen a street person? What was he or she wearing? Think about yourself dressed in the clothes of a street person—old, dirty, tattered, and stinking. These clothes are like your sins. Now think of someone just your size and shape wearing beautiful, expensive clothes of the finest fabric, from the most exclusive store. These clothes are like Jesus' goodness (righteousness). When Jesus died on the cross, he gave you his rich, royal robes and took your tattered rags.

Read—*2 Corinthians 5:21, 8:9*

God made him who had no sin to be sin for us, so that in him we might become the righteousness of God.

For you know the grace of our Lord Jesus Christ, that though he was rich, yet for your sakes he became poor, so that you through his poverty might become rich.

Discuss

1. These verses talk about several switches or trades. What are they?
2. When Jesus took our sin, what did we get?
3. How did Jesus become poor?
4. How did his poverty make us rich?

Final Thought

Our sin was destroyed on the cross. We are no longer wearing our smelly sin clothes. Instead, we are wearing Jesus' white robes of righteousness. That means that when God looks at us, he no longer sees our sin. Instead, he sees Jesus' goodness. We cannot do anything to earn it. This has already been done for us. All we must do is accept God's free gift.

Pray

Thank you, dear Lord, for trading places—for giving me your righteousness in exchange for my sins. I accept this gift that you offer me.

Sing—*Rock of Ages, Cleft for Me*

Nothing in my hand I bring; Simply to thy cross I cling.
Naked, come to thee for dress; Helpless, look to thee for grace;
Foul, I to the fountain fly; Wash me, Savior, or I die.

Do

Place the symbol of the two coats on your holiday tree.

Further Study for Adults

Read Romans 4:25, 5:6–11, 6:3–14. From these verses, what are some other "benefits of his passion?" Are these benefits a reality in your life? Why or why not?

Today we take another look at a wonderful effect of Jesus' death, but this look takes us into the future. Here we see a vision of what heaven will be like.

Read—Revelation 7:9–10, 13–17

After this I looked and there before me was a great multitude that no one could count, from every nation, tribe, people and language, standing before the throne and in front of the Lamb. They were wearing white robes and were holding palm branches in their hands. And they cried out in a loud voice:

"Salvation belongs to our God,
who sits on the throne,
and to the Lamb."

Then one of the elders asked me, "These in white robes—who are they, and where did they come from?"

I answered, "Sir, you know."

And he said, "These are they who have come out of the great tribulation; they have washed their robes and made them white in the blood of the Lamb. Therefore,

"they are before the throne of God
and serve him day and night in his temple;
and he who sits on the throne will spread his tent over them.
Never again will they hunger;
never again will they thirst.
The sun will not beat upon them,
nor any scorching heat.
For the Lamb at the center of the throne will be their shepherd;
he will lead them to springs of living water.
And God will wipe away every tear from their eyes."

Discuss
1. How is the multitude described? Who are they?
2. Who is the Lamb? What do we learn about him from these verses?
3. What is life going to be like now for these people?
4. What does it mean that the Lamb will be their shepherd?

Final Thought
Jesus is the spotless Lamb whose blood was shed as a sacrifice for our sins. He is also our Good Shepherd. He guides us, protects us, and cares for us. It is because of his sacrifice that we are able to go to heaven. And in heaven he will lead us and care for us in a way that is even more wonderful than we can imagine. Is the Lamb your shepherd today?

Pray
Lord Jesus, Lamb of God, wash away my sin. Lead me in your paths today.

Sing—*I Lay My Sins on Jesus*

I lay my sins on Jesus, The spotless Lamb of God;
He bears them all and frees us From the accursed load.
I bring my guilt to Jesus To wash my crimson stains
Clean in his blood most precious Till not a spot remains.

Do
Place the symbol of the radiant throne on your holiday tree.

Further Study for Adults
Read John 10:7–21. What does Jesus say about himself in these verses? What do these verses teach about Jesus and his death? How did others react to Jesus' words? What is your response? How do you recognize Jesus' voice? Would you say that you have life "to the full" (v. 10)?

Today is Maundy Thursday, the day that we remember Jesus' Last Supper with his disciples. Who can remember what special feast Jesus and his disciples were celebrating that night? Does your church have a special service on Maundy Thursday? We always have a service of Holy Communion, for it was at the Last Supper that Jesus took elements of the Passover meal and gave them new meaning. He gave believers a new feast, the feast of the bread and wine which stand for his blood shed for us and his body broken for us.

But what does "Maundy" mean? It comes from a Latin word which means commandment. It is called Maundy Thursday because at the Last Supper, Jesus gave his disciples a new commandment. This conversation took place after Judas left the Upper Room in order to go to the chief priests and betray Jesus. It was then that Jesus told his friends the important things he wanted them to remember.

Read—*John 13:33–38*

"My children, I will be with you only a little longer. You will look for me, and just as I told the Jews, so I tell you now: Where I am going, you cannot come.

"A new commandment I give you: Love one another. As I have loved you, so you must love one another. By this all men will know that you are my disciples, if you love one another."

Simon Peter asked him, "Lord, where are you going?"

Jesus replied, "Where I am going, you cannot follow now, but you will follow later."

Peter asked, "Lord, why can't I follow you now? I will lay down my life for you."

Then Jesus answered, "Will you really lay down your life for me? I tell you the truth, before the rooster crows, you will disown me three times!"

Discuss

1. What was Jesus' new commandment?
2. What made it new?
3. Where was Jesus going, that Peter could not follow right away?
4. What is the mark of the true disciple of Christ? By looking at your family relationships, can others tell that you are Christians? Why or why not?

Final Thought

Jesus showed us what love really is. He went to the cross for us. And he calls us to have that same kind of love for our Christian brothers and sisters. We are to set aside selfishness and work for the good of other Christians. When we begin to love with Christ's love, blessings ripple out to all whose lives touch ours—and beyond to countless others.

Pray

Dear Lord, thank you for showing us what love is. Help us to love as you have loved us.

Sing—*My Song Is Love Unknown*

My song is love unknown, My Savior's love to me,
Love to the loveless shown, That they might lovely be.
Oh, who am I, that for my sake
My Lord should take frail flesh and die?

Do

Place the symbol of the hands on your holiday tree.

Further Study for Adults

Read Ephesians 2:12–17. According to these verses, how did Jesus' death make the new commandment possible to obey? Paul is writing to nonJews here. What problems did they have before they knew Christ? What was Jesus' purpose? Peace means right relationships. With whom were the nonJews given new, right relationships? How has Christ affected your relationships?

Today is Good Friday, the day we remember Jesus' crucifixion. Have you ever wondered why it is called "Good" Friday? Jesus, who had done nothing wrong, died a horrible death on the cross. What's so good about that? The reason it is called Good Friday is that Jesus death was for our good. Because of his death, we are saved from death and sin. We who believe in him have eternal life and every good gift from God. Only Jesus' death could do this.

Before Jesus came and died, how were people forgiven their sins and made right with God? God set up a system which would point to Jesus. People were still saved by faith in God's provision. They were looking ahead to the cross, just as we look back to the cross by faith. The system that God set up was the system of high priests and sacrifices. Every day the high priest offered sacrifices at the temple. Blood was shed. The priest prayed for forgiveness for the people. The blood of goats, bulls, and sheep was not good enough to take away people's sin. But it pointed to Jesus' blood which was good enough. When Jesus died for us, he became both our great high priest and our sacrifice for sin.

Read—*Hebrews 7:23–26*

Now there have been many of those priests, since death prevented them from continuing in office; but because Jesus lives forever, he has a permanent priesthood. Therefore he is able to save completely those who come to God through him, because he always lives to intercede for them.

Such a high priest meets our need—one who is holy, blameless, pure, set apart from sins, exalted above the heavens. Unlike the other high priests, he does not need to offer sacrifices day after day, first for his own sins, and then for the sins of the people. He sacrificed for their sins once for all when he offered himself.

Discuss

1. How is Jesus different than the other priests?
2. Because Jesus was raised and lives forever, what is he able to do?
3. What need does Jesus meet, from these verses?
4. Why does Jesus not need to offer sacrifices day after day?

Final Thought

Ever since Adam and Eve, sin has been our big problem. Every bad thing in the world is the result of sin. Our need is for a solution to the sin problem. As our sacrifice, Jesus died to set us free from the penalty (punishment) of our sin. As our great high priest, Jesus was raised to live forever so that he can always continue to pray to the Father for us. This sets us free from the power of sin.

Pray

Thank you, Lord Jesus, that you are our sacrifice for sin and our great high priest.

Sing—*Christ the Lord Is Risen Today; Alleluia!*

For the sheep the Lamb has bled; Alleluia!
Sinless in the sinner's stead. Alleluia!
Christ the Lord is ris'n on high; Alleluia!
Now he lives, no more to die. Alleluia!

Do

Place the symbol of the cross on your holiday tree.

Further Study for Adults

Read Hebrews 9:11–15, 24–28. What contrasts do we find here? What further insights do these verses give concerning Christ's role as high priest and sacrifice? From these verses, what are the "benefits of his Passion?" What difference do these truths make in your life?

For Jesus' followers, the Sabbath day after his crucifixion was the most miserable day of their lives. Peter must have been tormented with guilt over his denial of Jesus. Mary and John probably comforted each other as they bitterly wept, grieving the loss of their beloved Jesus. The disciples banded together in secret for fear that the Jewish leaders would come after them next. They were confused, depressed, and deeply disappointed. Thomas was so depressed that he wouldn't even meet with the others. What a sad day!

But we don't need to be sad today, for we know the happy ending. Early on Sunday morning, Jesus was resurrected. He won the fight with Satan. Death could no longer touch him. We look forward to celebrating this glorious victory tomorrow!

Because of this victory, Jesus has great power and glory in heaven. Later, after Jesus had gone to heaven, he gave John a secret look at himself. This is what John saw:

Read—*Revelation 1:12–18*

I turned around to see the voice that was speaking to me. And when I turned I saw seven golden lampstands, and among the lampstands was someone "like a son of man," dressed in a robe reaching down to his feet and with a golden sash around his chest. His head and hair were white like wool, as white as snow, and his eyes were like blazing fire. His feet were like bronze glowing in a furnace, and his voice was like the sound of rushing waters. In his right hand he held seven stars, and out of his mouth came a sharp double-edged sword. His face was like the sun shining in all its brilliance.

When I saw him, I fell at his feet as though dead. Then he placed his right hand on me and said: "Do not be afraid. I am the First and the Last. I am the Living One; I was dead, and behold I am alive for ever and ever! And I hold the keys of death and Hades."

Discuss

1. Describe what John saw.
2. What did John do when he saw this vision of Jesus?
3. What did Jesus say about himself? What does this mean?
4. Does this vision change your image of Jesus? In what way?

Final Thought

The way Jesus is described is meant to tell us what he is like, not just how he is dressed. The long robe with golden sash tells us that he is our high priest. His white hair shows wisdom and honor. His blazing eyes show that he can see into people's hearts—that he understands everything. The sword coming out of his mouth means that as God he will judge everyone. Most important, his holding the keys of death and Hades means that he is in control even of death. He has all power, honor, and glory!

Pray

We praise you, Lord Christ! To you be praise and honor and glory and power, forever and ever!

Sing—*All Glory, Laud, and Honor*

All glory, laud, and honor To you, redeemer, king,
To whom the lips of children Made sweet hosannas ring.
The company of angels Are praising you on high;
Creation and all mortals In chorus make reply.

Do

Place the symbol of the two keys on your holiday tree.

Further Study for Adults

Read Revelation 5:6–14. Describe in your own words this vision of the glorified Christ. What various groups are praising the Lamb? Write down your personal reaction to these verses. Use the words to these prayers as your prayer of praise.

EASTER FAMILY
CELEBRATIONS

CELEBRATING EASTER: FAMILY WORSHIP
ON EASTER SUNDAY

The Christian tradition for Easter morning is to worship the risen Lord. This worship service is the climax of the entire church year. Going to church should be the highest priority for Easter Sunday. In addition to this, perhaps after the Easter dinner, a family worship time is appropriate. Here is a brief format for family worship on Easter.

Call to Worship
Leader: Alleluia. Christ is risen!
All: The Lord is risen, indeed! Alleluia!

Sing—*Jesus Christ Is Risen Today*

Jesus Christ is ris'n today, Alleluia!
Our triumphant holy day, Alleluia!
Who did once upon the cross, Alleluia!
Suffer to redeem our loss. Alleluia!

Hymns of praise, then, let us sing, Alleluia!
Unto Christ our heav'nly king, Alleluia!
Who endured the cross and grave, Alleluia!
Sinners to redeem and save, Alleluia!

But the pains which he endured, Alleluia!
Our salvation have procured, Alleluia!
Now above the sky he's king, Alleluia!
Where the angels ever sing, Alleluia!

Participate
Select one of the following Gospel accounts of the resurrection to act out. Props and costumes are unnecessary. Read the passage(s) over and try to perform faithfully the events as recorded in the Gospel.

Matthew 28:1–10

Mark 16:1–20
Luke 24:1–49
John 20:1–31

Discuss

Why was it important that Jesus be raised from the dead?

To answer this question, look up the following passages:
Acts 2:22–32
Romans 6:5–11
1 Corinthians 15:12–22
Ephesians 1:19–23

Pray

We praise you, O Christ, for the great power that you had to break the chains of death. Thank you that right now we can have new life in you, and someday we will have new bodies that will never die. In Jesus' name, Amen.

Sing—*Crown Him with Many Crowns*

Crown Him with many crowns, The Lamb upon his throne;
Hark! how the heav'nly anthem drowns All music but its own.
Awake, my soul, and sing Of him who died for thee,
And hail Him as thy matchless king Through all eternity.

Crown Him the Lord of love—Behold His hands and side,
Rich wounds yet visible above, In beauty glorified:
No angels in the sky Can fully bear that sight
But downward bend their burning eyes at mysteries so bright.

Crown Him the Lord of life, Who triumphed o'er the grave,
And rose victorious in the strife For those He came to save;
His glories now we sing, Who died and rose on high,
Who died eternal life to bring, And lives, that death may die.

CELEBRATING EASTER: HOLY TREASURE HUNT

The entire family will enjoy preparing for and participating in this exciting Easter game.

The Holy Treasure Hunt can be used instead of or in addition to the usual Easter egg hunt. The hidden "treasures" are objects from the passages the family has been reading (e.g. a bottle of perfume to represent Jesus' anointing at Bethany). This is a fun way to review and reinforce all that the children have learned.

PREPARATION

Involve the children in collecting and making the items to be used. Some are ordinary household items (bottle of perfume, sponge), others will have to be made of paper, wood, or whatever materials you have on hand. When the children are in bed or are in another room, hide the items.

Items

The following correspond to Lenten Devotions:

picture of a door (corresponds to devotion on p. 20)

picture of a roast turkey (corresponds to devotion on p. 22)

picture of praying hands (corresponds to devotion on p. 24)

picture of a camel (corresponds to devotion on p. 26)

jar of spices (corresponds to devotion on p. 28)

picture of eyes (corresponds to devotion on p. 30)

branch from a tree (corresponds to devotion on p. 32)

perfume bottle (corresponds to devotion on p. 34)

figure of a colt (corresponds to devotion on p. 36)

coat (corresponds to devotion on p. 38)

stone (corresponds to devotion on p. 40)

running shoe (corresponds to devotion on p. 42)

doll-sized table (corresponds to devotion on p. 44)

dried grapevine (corresponds to devotion on p. 46)

dollar bill (corresponds to devotion on p. 48)

two pennies (corresponds to devotion on p. 50)

heart (corresponds to devotion on p. 52)

water jug (corresponds to devotion on p. 54)
gardening spade ((corresponds to devotion on p. 56)
towel (corresponds to devotion on p. 58)
wine glass (corresponds to devotion on p. 60)
stick (shepherd's staff) (corresponds to devotion on p. 62)
cup (corresponds to devotion on p. 64)
lipstick print on a tissue (corresponds to devotion on p. 66)
picture of a rooster (corresponds to devotion on p. 68)
Bible (corresponds to devotion on p. 70)
old belt (corresponds to devotion on p. 72)
thirty nickels (corresponds to devotion on p. 74)
construction paper crown (corresponds to devotion on p. 76)
hammer (corresponds to devotion on p. 78)
thorny branch twisted into a circlet (corresponds to devotion on p. 80)
cross (corresponds to devotion on p. 82)
pair of glasses (corresponds to devotion on p. 84)
sign reading "THE KING OF THE JEWS" (corresponds to devotion on p. 86)
heart or valentine (corresponds to devotion on p. 88)
sponge (corresponds to devotion on p. 90)
curtain fabric (corresponds to devotion on p. 92)
strip of linen (corresponds to devotion on p. 94)
lock (corresponds to devotion on p. 96)
palm branch (corresponds to devotion on p. 98)
two keys (corresponds to devotion on p. 110)

Note: these are a lot of items, and some of them are difficult to connect with the Bible story! If you have older children, they will enjoy the challenge. For families with only small children, hide only about ten of the more obvious items.

TO PLAY

1. Have the children go on a hunt to find the items. Because they were involved in the preparation, they know exactly what they are seeking.

2. When all the items have been located and gathered up, come back together and have the children show what they have found.

3. As each item is displayed, ask the children what part that item played in the events of Holy Week ("Do you remember a sponge in anything we read this week?")

4. If your children can read and are stumped on any of the items, give them the Bible reference as a clue. Let them look it up in the Bible and figure it out.

FAMILY
CELEBRATIONS
AT
EASTER

PASSOVER CELEBRATION

CELEBRATING PASSOVER: INTRODUCTION

O f all the family celebrations of the year, Passover is my very favorite. We experienced our first Messianic Passover cele-bration about fourteen years ago in our own home, led by our friend Chris Barnekov. While none of us present was Jewish, we all loved the richness of the symbolism. Chris explained as we went along how each part of the service pointed to Christ and was fulfilled in his death and resurrection. Light bulbs started going off inside of me. With each new revelation, my excitement grew until I could hardly sit still.

Passover became one of our family traditions. This past spring we celebrated Passover with our friends, Steve and Kathy Friedberg and their two children, Ben and Elaine. Steve is a Messianic Jew, a Jewish person who believes that Yeshua (Jesus) is the Messiah. It was a wonderful celebration, fun, meaningful, and enlightening. I am so grateful to Steve for his invaluable assistance in this Passover portion of the book. He brought to this project his knowledge of Jewish tradition and the Hebrew language, as well as his thoughtful insights into the relationship between Jewish faith and tradition and the fulfillment of these in Jesus Christ.

"Why Celebrate Passover? I'm a Christian!"
Every Christian home can be enriched by celebrating Passover, just as our Lord did. For Jesus, Passover was the most significant of holy days. Because of Jesus' death and resurrection, we too can join in cel-ebrating this wonderful feast. In fact, for Christians, Passover is even more significant, because it finds its fulfillment in Jesus. It was no accident that Jesus was crucified at Passover. He became the once for all Sacrifice which allows God's judgment to "pass over" us.

Passover demonstrates God's unifying purpose throughout history. Jesus was not God's Plan B. From the very beginning, God purposed to send Jesus, the second person of the Trinity, to be the sacrifice for our sin. This is abundantly clear as we go through the *seder* (pro-nounced SAY-der, which means "prescribed order") or the Passover ceremony. In the *seder*, we reflect upon how God delivered his peo-ple from slavery in Egypt. Each part of the *seder* points also to Jesus as the means by which God has delivered us from slavery to sin.

A typical Jewish *seder* will not make that connection, of course. But those of us who have come to faith in Jesus see the significance of these things, especially because it was the Passover which Jesus was celebrating with his disciples in the upper room on the night that he was betrayed. It was the middle matzah which Jesus broke and proclaimed, "This is my body given for you." It was the third cup of wine, the Cup of Redemption, that Jesus lifted up when he said, "This cup is the new covenant in my blood, which is poured out for you." When one understands what Jesus was saying with these Passover elements, the significance is staggering. Christians cannot fully understand and appreciate Holy Communion until we have celebrated Passover. Only then do we know what Jesus was saying to his disciples on that night.

One of the things I enjoy about Passover is that it has not become commercialized, as have so many Christian holidays. With most holidays, we find ourselves fighting against an onslaught of cultural images and expectations as we try to preserve the spiritual essence of the celebration. Not so with Passover. Passover is untainted by these secular contaminants. It is purely religious.

Why not celebrate Passover? Even at face value, Passover commemorates something in which we as Christians believe—God's mighty work of deliverance for his people. If we have Jewish friends and neighbors, our observance of Passover can be a bridge or point of contact. Through it, we can better understand and communicate with our Jewish friends.

Besides, it's fun! In one single event, Passover combines most of the ingredients of a wonderful celebration:

family and friends gathered together,
good food,
rich spiritual significance and biblical truth,
meaningful traditions, rituals, and song.

Passover is meant to be celebrated in the home, with family and close friends. It is a celebration which includes and involves everyone, from the youngest to the oldest. Because it employs all the senses, it is a hands-on experience which the children will enjoy. It is the ideal "family celebration!"

Passover—a Holiday with a History

The celebration of Passover was instituted by God as a commemoration of his mighty deliverance of the people of Israel from slavery in Egypt. God commanded the Israelites to observe this feast every year. In Exodus 12, we read of God's instructions to Moses concerning this celebration. Thousands of years have passed, and still the Jewish people observe this feast. The intervening years have brought additions and traditions to the outline that God gave Moses.

The modern day Passover *seder* has many variations. This is my own version. I have written it with Christian families in mind—families with children of various ages.

"What, Gentiles observe Passover? You've got nerve!"

You will notice that throughout the *seder*, God's people the Israelites are referred to as "we" rather than "they." There is a very important reason for this. In Exodus 13:8, God instructed Moses and the Israelites to "tell your son, 'I do this because of what the Lord did for me when I came out of Egypt.'" It was essential for succeeding generations to know that they also were delivered from slavery by God's own provision. God wanted their children and their children's children to identify with their forefathers.

What about us Gentile Christians? What right do we have to identify with the Israelites?

Did you know that believing Gentiles were included when the Israelites fled from Egypt? Exodus 12:38 says that "many other people went up with them." Later in that same chapter, the Lord gave Passover instructions for aliens living among the Israelites.

We who believe in the God of Abraham, Isaac and Jacob have every right to participate in the feast of Passover. Indeed, if we place our faith in Jesus Christ, we are Abraham's spiritual children. Romans 4:16 tells us: "Therefore, the promise comes by faith, so that it may be by grace and may be guaranteed to all Abraham's offspring—not only to those who are of the law but also to those who are of the faith of Abraham. He is the father of us all."

As children of Abraham, then, "Let us keep the feast!"

CELEBRATING PASSOVER: PREPARATION FOR THE *SEDER*

As with any special occasion, Passover requires preparation. Jesus sent his disciples into Jerusalem to make preparations for this celebration (Luke 22:7–13). In fact, Luke devoted seven verses to the subject of the Passover preparations.

Fortunately, Passover is not expensive to celebrate, nor does it need to be an excessive amount of work. It does involve shopping for several food items that one does not normally buy and preparing these dishes. The foods may be different, but they are not complicated.

Traditionally, the preparation of the food and the table have fallen on the woman of the house. The eldest male present at the *seder* then leads the ceremony. This is often the father or the grandfather.

Times have changed, and in today's family, anyone can help with the preparations. In the actual *seder* ceremony, however, the roles continue to be distinct and separate. The woman of the house lights the candles. The eldest male leads the ceremony. Tradition is what it is all about!

Be sure to involve your children in the preparations for Passover. Even tiny children can help make chicken soup by adding the ingredients that you have measured or chopped. Older children will enjoy taking greater responsibility—they can mix, chop, measure, pour, etc. You will find the preparations are half the fun when it becomes a family project!

Here are instructions for preparing for the Passover celebration, beginning with important terms. I have tried to keep it uncomplicated, but to include everything you need to know in order to prepare and celebrate a Messianic Passover *seder*.

Terms

afikomen (ah-fee-KOH-men) it has come to mean dessert, but its origin is a Greek word which some believe means "He who comes."

charoseth (hah-ROH-seth) a mixture made of chopped apples, nuts, and wine (recipe follows) *dayenu* (die-AY-noo) "It would have been enough for us."

haggadah (hah-GAH-dah) literally, "to tell." It is the written passages and rituals used in the *seder* service. Each person around the *seder* table has a copy of the words used in the service. These pages are called the *haggadah*.

karpas (KAR-pas) parsley (celery may be substituted)

maror (mah-ROAR) bitter herbs, specifically horseradish

matzah (MAHT-zah) large Jewish cracker-like bread made without yeast. There is no substitute for real matzah. You can buy it in most grocery stores at this time of year. If they do not have it, try a delicatessen.

seder (SAY-der) literally, prescribed order. This is the word for the Passover service or liturgy.

Yeshua (yeh-SHOO-ah) Jesus

The *Seder* Plate

Essential to the celebration of Passover is the *seder* plate—a large plate in the center of the table which holds the symbols of Passover. Here are the items that you will need:

Lamb's shankbone—Can be obtained from butcher. Remove the meat and roast the bone in the oven until dry and brown. It can be stored and reused in subsequent years.

Parsley—One sprig per person

Horseradish—Ground but not creamed. Preferably red. One teaspoon per person.

Charoseth—Apple-Nut Mixture. Here's the recipe:

> 1 tart apple, peeled, cored, &
> chopped or grated
> 1/2 cup chopped walnuts
> 1/8 tsp. cinnamon
> 1 tsp. honey or sugar
> 1 tbsp. wine or grape juice
> Mix together and refrigerate. It is supposed
> to turn brown. Serves 5 to 8 people.

Salt water—One cup for dipping the parsley.

Roasted Egg—Egg should not be boiled but roasted in the oven. This is to represent the roasting of the sacrifice at the Temple. Poke a hole in one end with a pin to prevent it from exploding in the oven. Roast it until it is golden brown.

The Unity

This too is a necessary part of the *seder*. It is a plate holding three matzot (plural for matzah) inside one napkin and covered with a second napkin.

For the Unity, you will need:

> One large dinner plate
> Two dinner-sized napkins
> Three full-sized unbroken matzot

To prepare the Unity, the three whole matzot are placed within different sections of one folded napkin. Then the second napkin is unfolded and draped over the top.

During the *seder*, the middle matzah will be broken in two. One half is returned to the middle of the Unity and the other half is wrapped in the top napkin and hidden by the leader. After the meal, the children find the hidden matzah (or *afikomen*), and it is ransomed by the father. Not only is this great fun for the children, but it is highly significant. The meaning will be explained by the leader at the appropriate time during the *seder*. The explanation is in the *Haggadah*.

The *Seder* Table

Add these special features to your holiday table setting:

Candles
The two candles are both at the end of the table occupied by the woman of the house. (At the opposite end of the table sits the leader, who is the eldest male.)

Pillows
Each chair should have a pillow on which the person can lean back.

Elijah's Place
Set an extra place for Elijah the prophet. This is a Jewish tradition and will be discussed during the *seder*.

Wine Glasses
Each place setting must have a wine glass. You may use wine (red or blush), nonalcoholic wine, or grape juice. For simplicity's sake, I simply refer to it as "wine" and "the cup." Place the bottle or pitcher near the leader. He will do the pouring as a part of the *seder*. Each person will drain his or her cup four times during the *seder*. For that reason, I recommend that when the leader "fills" the cups, he puts in only an ounce or so.

Handwashing Bowl
You may pass one basin around the table, with a towel, or you may place small fingertip bowls full of water on the table for every two people to share.

The *Haggadah*

Make enough copies of the *Haggadah* (pp. 134–150 of this book), collate and staple them, so that each person has his or her own copy. Place this to the left of the forks at each place setting.

The *Seder* Plate

This occupies the center of the table and must be within reach of the leader. Everything should be on the *seder* plate, as directed above, when the family is called to the table.

The Unity

Assemble the Unity as directed above, and place this to the right of the leader.

The Passover Meal

Instructions for the Passover meal, including a menu, may be found on p. 130.

Now you are ready to celebrate Passover!

My prayer is that your family, like mine, will love the Passover celebration, and through celebrating this wonderful feast, you will together draw near to our Passover sacrifice, the Lamb of God, Yeshua the Messiah.

"Christ our Passover is sacrificed for us;

Therefore let us keep the feast." (The Book of Common Prayer)

THE PASSOVER MEAL

Midway through the *seder*, the passover meal is eaten. Allow forty-five minutes for the first portion of the *seder*. Do not have any food on the table during this time except the *seder* plate, the unity, and the wine. The meal should be "on hold" in the kitchen.

What does one eat at Passover? For many years, because we celebrated this feast with another Christian family, I served an ordinary holiday meal. Now, however, I want to go the whole nine yards and prepare the meal that Jewish families eat at Passover. The unique meal makes the holiday that much more distinctive. You may want to compromise and simply eliminate any yeast and leaven from your meal. I would also suggest that you not serve pork or ham. But why not have some fun and eat what Jewish families all over the world eat on this night?

Jewish families serve one of several traditional meals. Because the laws concerning what may be eaten, particularly at Passover, are so restrictive, these traditional meals are quite specific.

Lamb is not served in a Jewish home on Passover anymore because there is no longer a temple where sacrifices are being offered. If you should invite a Jewish friend to your *seder* and you served lamb, your Jewish friend would immediately leave your home, offended. And don't even think about serving pork or ham! Dairy products are also taboo, because of regulations prohibiting the eating of dairy products together with meat. (Margarine is okay if it is made with corn oil.) Peas and beans are not allowed, as well. The biggest no-no is leaven. To be safe, look for the kosher symbol (Ⓚ) on the food package. All food must be prepared with matzah or matzah flour where you would have used bread or regular flour.

As you can see, these restrictions severely limit your options. If you want to be kosher, here is a sample of what you MAY serve at Passover:

Menu for the Passover Meal

Tossed Green Salad (no croutons, bacon, or dairy-base dressing)
Chicken Soup with Matzah Ball (recipe follows)

Roasted Chicken, Beef, or Turkey
Boiled Potatoes with Parsley or Roasted Potatoes
Honeyed Carrots
Applesauce or Fresh Fruit
Macaroons (buy these at your store or Jewish community center)
Coffee/Tea

Our grocery store carries a full line of kosher products, including mixes for many of these and other Passover foods. If your store does not carry these, ask the store manager. He could order them for you. Otherwise, you may call a nearby synagogue or Jewish community center for assistance in finding the food items you need. Also, at this time of year, many stores and delis sell ready-made kosher foods.

Recipe for Chicken Soup with Matzah Ball *(serves eight)*

Chicken Soup (Day before or morning of seder)

1 whole, large chicken, 4-5 pounds, cleaned thoroughly
3 quarts cold water
2 onions, sliced
3 carrots, sliced
2 stalks of celery, including tops
1 tablespoon salt
1/2 teaspoon garlic powder
1/4 teaspoon pepper
1 bay leaf

Bring all ingredients to a boil in a large covered kettle. Lower heat and simmer for 3 hours. Pour soup through colander and refrigerate broth for 2–3 hours or overnight, until a solid layer of fat forms on the top. Remove the layer of fat (save this for the matzah balls). Reheat broth 1–2 hours before serving, adding matzah balls during this time. This yields 2 to 2–1/2 quarts of soup.

Matzah Balls (Day before or morning of seder)

1 cup matzah meal
1/2 cup water
1/3 cup vegetable oil or chicken fat
4 eggs
1 teaspoon salt

Beat eggs and mix in oil or fat. In a separate bowl, mix together salt and matzah meal. Add dry ingredients to egg mixture, blending thoroughly. Stir in water. Cover and refrigerate for 1 hour. Bring a pot of slightly salted water to a rolling boil. Take matzah batter from refrigerator and lightly form the batter into meatball-sized balls. The batter will be sticky and hard to work with. The trick is to avoid handling and compacting the balls. It's okay if they are only roughly shaped lumps. Immediately after forming each ball, gently drop it into the boiling water. (The balls should first sink, then rise to the surface.) Reduce heat, cover and simmer for about 45 minutes. Remove from water, cover, and refrigerate until 1–2 hours before serving. Add matzah balls to chicken broth as it reheats. Keep warm on stove during the first part of the *seder*.

Just prior to the *seder*, put the chicken soup on the stove to warm during the first part of *seder*. Add the matzah balls to the soup. Serve the soup before the main course.

For more Passover recipes, mixes, and prepared foods, write to:

Aron Streit Inc.
148–154 Rivington Street
New York, NY 10002

Deborah Ross
The B. Manischewitz Company
Box 484A
Jersey City, NJ 07303-0484

Have a blessed Passover!

PASSOVER FOR CHRISTIANS

CELEBRATING PASSOVER: THE *SEDER*

The Candles
Leader *(eldest male of the family)*
As we light these candles tonight, we pray that God will light our hearts with his Holy Spirit. We want to understand how God has redeemed his people.

The woman of the house *(lighting the candles)*
Blessed are you, O Lord our God, King of the universe. You have made us your own. We light these festival lights in your Name.

The Four Cups of Wine
Leader
When we were slaves in Egypt, God heard our cries. He chose Moses to lead us out of Egypt. These are the four promises that God made to Moses.

Reader 1
   "I will bring you out from under the yoke of the Egyptians."

Reader 2
   "I will free you from being slaves."

Reader 3
   "I will redeem you with an outstretched arm."

Reader 4
   "I will take you as my own people, and I will be your God."

Leader
We remember these four promises at Passover by drinking from our cups four times. The first is called the Cup of Sanctification, the second, the Cup of the Plagues, the third, the Cup of Redemption, and the fourth, the Cup of Praise.

The Cup of Sanctification

Leader (*pouring wine into each cup*)
(If you elect to fill the cup each time, instruct the family to drink only one sip when it is time to drink the cup. If you want to drain the cup each time, pour only a small amount into the cups each time you are to fill them.)
This is the Cup of Sanctification or setting apart as holy.

Reader 1
"I will bring you out from under the yoke of the Egyptians."

Family (*lifting their cups*)
Blessed are you, O Lord our God, King of the universe, who creates the fruit of the vine. (All drink.)

The Hand Washing

Leader
We wash our hands to remind us that God is holy. As we come before him, we too must be holy. As it is written:

Reader 4
"Who may ascend the hill of the Lord? Who may stand in his holy place? He who has clean hands and a pure heart." (Psalm 24:3,4)

Leader (*lifting the basin of water*)
Let us share together in this hand washing ceremony.
(Pass the bowl. Each person dips his hands and passes bowl to next person.)

Leader
Let us also remember how Yeshua (yeh-SHOO-ah, or Jesus) took off his clothes and, wearing a towel, washed the feet of his disciples. In doing this, he showed that he came as a humble servant. We know

that this water cannot really make our hearts clean. The only way that our hearts can be made pure and holy is by Yeshua's greatest act of servanthood, his death on the cross.

The Karpas (pronounced KAR-pas)

Leader
We now remember the tears of our people when we were slaves in Egypt. As it is written:

Reader 2
"The Israelites groaned in their slavery and cried out, and their cry for help because of their slavery went up to God." (Exodus 2:23)

Leader *(lifting the parsley)(Celery may be substituted for parsley)*
Passover comes in the spring, when we see new life around us. The *karpas*, or parsley, reminds us that life is a gift to us from our great and mighty God. The *karpas* is also like the hyssop plant which our forefathers used to smear the blood of the lamb on the door frame.

(lifting the salt water)
When we were slaves in Egypt, life was not easy. It was full of pain, suffering, and tears. This salt water stands for our tears.

Family *(dipping their parsley in salt water)*
Blessed are you, O Lord our God, King of the universe, who creates the fruit of the earth. (All eat *karpas*.)

The Breaking of the Middle Matzah

Leader *(lifting the Unity, or the plate which holds the three matzot wrapped in napkins)*
At Passover, three matzot are wrapped together. They are called the "Unity." Jewish teachers have many explanations for this. We who know Yeshua look at the Unity and see God the Father, God the Son, and God the Holy Spirit.

(Leader takes the middle matzah out of the Unity, breaks it in two, replaces one half and wraps the other half in a linen cloth for the afikomen.)

I have taken the middle matzah and broken it in half. One half is wrapped and hidden. This is called the *afikomen* (pronounced ah-fee-KOH-men), and it is an important part of the *seder* which comes after the meal. (hides the *afikomen*)

The Four Questions

Leader

We now ask and answer the four questions. As it is written:

Reader 3

"When your children ask you, 'What does this ceremony mean to you?' then tell them." (Exodus 12:26)

A Young Child

Why is this night different from all other nights?

1) On all other nights, we eat leavened bread.
   On this night, why do we eat only matzah, or unleavened bread?

2) On all other nights, we eat all kinds of vegetables.
   On this night, why do we eat only bitter herbs?

3) On all other nights, we do not dip our vegetables even once.
   On this night, why do we dip them twice?

4) On all other nights, we eat our meals sitting.
   On this night, why do we eat only reclining?

Leader

God has commanded us to answer these questions for our children. But we do so with thankful hearts, for the answers point to the great and mighty works of God.

Leader *(lifting one matzah)*

On all other nights we eat leavened bread, but on Passover we eat only matzah. This reminds us that when we fled from Egypt, we did not have time to let the bread rise. Yeshua often compared yeast, which makes bread rise, with sin. He came to die and take away our sin.

Leader (*lifting the maror, pronounced mah-ROAR*)
On all other nights we eat all kinds of vegetables, but on Passover we eat only *maror*, or bitter herbs. This reminds us of how bitter life was for us in Egypt. It also reminds us of life in slavery to sin.

Leader (*lifting the charoseth, pronounced hah-ROH-seth*)
On all other nights we do not dip our vegetables even once, but tonight we dip them twice. We have already dipped our parsley in salt water. Now we will dip our bitter herbs into sweet kharoset. This mixture reminds us of the mortar and bricks which we were forced to make as slaves in Egypt.

Leader
On all other nights we eat sitting up, but tonight we eat reclining. This is to remind us that now we are free from slavery. On the first Passover, we had to eat in a hurry, with our coats and sandals on, holding our staffs in our hands as we waited to be delivered from slavery. Now we may relax and enjoy this feast at our leisure.

The Story of Passover

Leader
Now we tell the story of Passover.

Reader 1
Long ago, the Lord brought Abraham to the land of Canaan. God promised Abraham that this land would belong to his descendants. Abraham's grandson Jacob left that land and moved with his family to Egypt to escape a famine. Jacob's family grew, becoming our people, the Israelites. Several hundred years passed, and by this time, we had become a huge nation. The Pharoah, or ruler of Egypt,

feared that we would join Egypt's enemies and fight against Egypt. So Pharoah decided to make us his slaves. Even so, God blessed us with more and more children.

Reader 2
This made the Pharoah even more nervous. He ordered his soldiers to throw every boy baby into the Nile River. One Israelite family hid their baby for three months. When they could hide him no longer, they put him in a basket and floated it out on the Nile River with his sister Miriam watching over him. The daughter of Pharoah found the basket and decided to keep the baby and raise him as her own son. She named him Moses, which means "drawn from the water."

Reader 3
Even though Moses grew up in Pharoah's court, he knew that he was an Israelite. He saw how we were mistreated by the Egyptians. One day, when he saw an Egyptian being cruel to an Israelite, Moses lost his temper and killed the Egyptian. He ran away from Egypt into a desert land where he worked as a shepherd.

Reader 4
The Lord heard our cries as we suffered at the hands of the Egyptians. He came to Moses in a burning bush and told Moses to go to Pharoah. Moses was afraid, but he finally agreed that with the help of his brother, Aaron, he would go to Pharoah and deliver God's message to "Let my people go!"

The Cup of Plagues

Leader
Pharoah did not want to let our people go. Every time Pharoah said no to Moses, God sent a plague or disaster to Pharoah and the land of Egypt. But Pharoah hardened his heart and kept saying no. The tenth time, God sent the most awful plague. This plague caused Pharoah to change his mind.

Family

"On that same night I will pass through Egypt and strike down every firstborn—both men and animals—and I will bring judgment on all the gods of Egypt; I am the Lord." (Exodus 12:12)

Leader

It was the Lord himself who passed over us and struck down the firstborn of the Egyptians. In this way he delivered us from slavery. As it is written:
On that same night I will pass through Egypt.

Family

I, and not an angel.

Leader

and strike down every firstborn—both men and animals—

Family

I, and not a seraph.

Leader

and I will bring judgment on all the gods of Egypt;

Family

I, and not a messenger.

Leader

I am the Lord.

Family

I myself and none other. (Exodus 12:12)

Leader *(filling the cups)*

We fill our cups a second time to remember that many people died during the plagues, especially the last one, in order that God's people would be set free. We also remember what it cost for us to be set free from sin and death—the lifeblood of Yeshua. As it is written:

Reader 2:
"I will free you from being slaves."

Leader
Each of the plagues focused on a being that the Egyptians worshipped. As we say each plague, we dip our finger into the cup and drip the liquid onto our plate. Think about how God showed himself much greater than all the false gods of Egypt.

Family *(each plague is said loudly in unison while dipping a finger and letting a drop of wine fall onto the plate)*
BLOOD! FROGS! GNATS! FLIES! CATTLE DISEASE! BOILS! HAIL! LOCUSTS! DARKNESS! DEATH OF THE FIRSTBORN!
(Do not drink the cup yet.)

The Dayenu
(pronounced die-AY-noo, meaning "it would have been sufficient")

Leader
God has been so good to us! We do not deserve his great and numerous blessings. Any one of his acts of mercy would have been enough to show his love for us.

Reader 1
With lovingkindness he redeemed us from Egypt, bringing judgment on the Egyptians and their gods.

Family
Dayenu.

Reader 2
With awesome power he divided the Red Sea, allowing us to pass over in safety.

Family
Dayenu.

Reader 3
With tender care he protected us in the wilderness, feeding us with manna and providing for our needs.

Family
Dayenu.

Reader 4
With great goodness he gave us the Law on Mt. Sinai.
With triumph he led us into the promised land of Israel.

Family *(lifting their cups)*
Dayenu! How many are your great blessings to us. For each act of goodness we are abundantly grateful. Most of all, we are thankful for Yeshua the Messiah. In him we have forgiveness of sins and abundant and everlasting life. Hallelujah! *(**Drink the second cup of wine.**)*

The Passover Lamb

Leader *(lifting the shankbone of the lamb)*
This shankbone of lamb reminds us of the lamb that each Israelite family killed on the night of the first Passover. God commanded that we take the blood of the lamb and put it on the top and the sides of the door frame of their house. As it is written:

Reader 1
"Then they are to take some of the blood and put it on the sides and tops of the door frames of the houses where they eat the lambs." (Exodus 12:7)

Reader 2
"That same night they are to eat the meat roasted over the fire, along with bitter herbs and bread made without yeast." (Exodus 12:8)

Reader 3
"This is how you are to eat it: with your cloak tucked into your belt, your

sandals on your feet and your staff in your hand. Eat it in haste; it is the Lord's Passover." (Exodus 12:11)

Reader 4

"The blood will be a sign for you on the houses where you are; and when I see the blood, I will pass over you. No destructive plague will touch you when I strike Egypt." (Exodus 12:13)

Leader

We who trust in Yeshua the Messiah believe that he is our Passover lamb. Just as it was God himself who redeemed the Israelites, so it is God himself, in the person of Yeshua the Messiah, who redeemed us once and for all from sin and death. He is the Lamb of God who takes away the sin of the world.

Leader (*lifting the roasted egg*)

This roasted egg is a special Passover offering. It is a symbol of mourning, reminding us of the destruction of the Temple in Jerusalem. It is also a sign of new and eternal life. It is because of Yeshua, our Passover lamb, that we can have eternal life.

The Matzah

Leader (*lifts the Unity*)

Family

Blessed are you, O Lord our God, King of the universe, who brings forth bread from the earth.

Leader (*takes the middle matzah from the unity, breaks it into olive size pieces, and distributes it to the family*)

Let us now share the unleavened bread of Passover.

Family (*holding the piece of matzah*)

Blessed are you, O Lord our God, King of the universe. You set us apart as your people and commanded us to eat unleavened bread. (*All eat.*)

The Maror

Leader (*Pass horseradish. Each person scoops some onto a piece of matzah.*)

Family (*lifting matzah with bitter herbs*)
Blessed are you, O Lord our God, King of the universe, who has set us apart by your Word and commanded us to eat bitter herbs. (*All eat.*)

Leader
The bitter herb reminds us of our persecution and suffering under the cruel hand of Pharoah. Just as the horseradish brings tears to our eyes now, so then did our great suffering bring tears to our eyes.

The Charoseth

Leader (*Takes two pieces from the bottom matzah and puts between them the charoseth, in a sandwich-like fashion. Pass charoseth. Each person scoops charoseth onto a piece of matzah.*)

Leader
The *charoseth* reminds us of the mortar and clay bricks that we made as slaves in Egypt. (*All eat.*)

Leader
It was at this point in the Passover *seder* that Yeshua told his disciples that one of them would betray him. When each asked, "Surely, not I?" Yeshua said that it was the one who dipped his bread into the bowl with Yeshua.

The Passover Supper
(*Leader offers prayer of thanks for the meal. Supper is served and eaten.*)

The Eating of the Afikomen

(After the meal, the children hunt for the afikomen, the wrapped and hidden matzah from the Unity. The leader ransoms it back by paying money to the child who finds it.)

Leader *(unwrapping the matzah and showing the family)*
We call this the *afikomen*, a Greek word. Jewish tradition has it that *afikomen* means dessert, but some scholars believe it comes from a root word which means "I have come." Yeshua called himself the bread of life. As it is written:

Reader 1
"Then Jesus declared, 'I am the bread of life. He who comes to me will never go hungry.'"

Reader 2
"'I am the living bread that came down from heaven. If anyone eats of this bread, he will live forever. This bread is my flesh, which I will give for the life of the world.'"

Reader 3
"'Whoever eats my flesh and drinks my blood has eternal life, and I will raise him up at the last day.'"

Reader 4
"'Your forefathers ate manna and died, but he who feeds on this bread will live forever.'" (John 6:35a, 51, 54, 58b)

Leader
The matzah is a picture for us of Yeshua and what he did for us. Look at how the matzah is striped. As it is written:

Family
"But he was wounded for our transgressions, he was bruised for our iniquities: the chastisement of our peace was upon him; and with his stripes we are healed." (Isaiah 53:5)

Leader

Look at how the matzah is pierced. As it is written:

Family

"They shall look upon me whom they have pierced." (Zechariah 12:10b)

Leader

See how the matzah is unleavened. Leaven stands for sin. Just as this bread is without leaven, Jesus was without sin. As it is written:

Family

"He committed no sin, and no deceit was found in his mouth." (Isaiah 53:9, 1 Peter 2:22)

Leader

The middle matzah from the Unity was broken, just as Yeshua, the Messiah was broken with suffering and death. We wrapped it in a white cloth, just as Yeshua's body was wrapped in linen cloth for burial. Just as the *afikomen* was hidden, so Yeshua's body was hidden for a short time in the grave. Just as the *afikomen* was brought out of hiding, so Yeshua arose from the grave.

Leader (*lifting the afikomen*)

Family

Blessed are you, O Lord our God, King of the universe, who brings forth bread from the earth.

Leader (*breaking the afikomen and distributing it to all*)

It was then that Yeshua added, "This is my body given for you; do this in remembrance of me" (Luke 22:19). Let us now eat matzah, remembering the broken body of the Lamb of God who takes away the sin of the world. (***All eat.***)

The Cup of Redemption

Leader *(filling the cups)*
Now we fill our cups a third time. *(lifting the cup)* This is the cup of redemption. It stands for the blood of the Passover lamb. As it is written:

Reader 3
"I will redeem you with an outstretched arm."

Leader
It was this cup, the cup of redemption, that Yeshua took after supper, saying, "This cup is the new covenant in my blood, which is poured out for you" (Luke 22:20). Just as the blood of the Passover lamb provided salvation for us in Egypt, so Yeshua's blood provides eternal salvation to all who believe.

Family *(lifting their cups)*
Blessed are you, O Lord our God, King of the universe, who creates the fruit of the vine. Let us drink with thankful hearts, remembering the Messiah's sacrifice for us.

The Prophet Elijah

Leader *(lifting the extra cup from Elijah's place)*
This cup is for Elijah the Prophet. In Jewish tradition, one of the children opens the door to see if Elijah will come to the *seder*. As it is written:

Family
"See, I will send you the prophet Elijah before that great and terrible day of the Lord comes." (Malachi 4:5)

Leader
We who believe in Yeshua believe that Elijah has already come. Yeshua spoke of John the Baptist as the Elijah who was to come, and

it was John who said, "Look, the Lamb of God, who takes away the sin of the world!" (John 1:29). We set this place for Elijah to recognize that he has come in the person of John the Baptist.

The Cup of Praise

Leader *(filling the cups)*
Now we fill our cups for the fourth and final time. This is the cup of praise. We praise him especially because of his promise to us:

Reader 4
"I will take you as my people and I will be your God." (Exodus 6:7)

Leader *(lifting the cup)*
With the cup of praise, we give thanks to God in the words of a psalm, just as Yeshua did with his disciples. After each phrase of thanksgiving, the family will join in saying, "His love endures forever."

Leader: Give thanks to the Lord, for he is good.
Family: His love endures forever.

Leader: Give thanks to the God of gods.
Family: His love endures forever.

Leader: Give thanks to the Lord of lords:
Family: His love endures forever.

Leader: to him who alone does great wonders,
Family: His love endures forever.

Leader: to him who struck down the firstborn of Egypt
Family: His love endures forever.

Leader: and brought Israel out from among them
Family: His love endures forever.

Leader: with a mighty hand and outstretched arm;
Family: His love endures forever.

Leader: to the One who remembered us in our low estate
Family: His love endures forever.

Leader: and freed us from our enemies,
Family: His love endures forever.

Leader: and who gives food to every creature.
Family: His love endures forever.

Leader: Give thanks to the God of heaven.
Family: His love endures forever.

Leader
Lifting our cups, let us bless the name of the Lord together.

Family (*lifting their cups*)
Blessed are you, O Lord our God, King of the universe, who creates the fruit of the vine. (*All drink.*)

Leader
The prescribed order of the Passover service is now complete. May we remember throughout the year that our redemption is complete by the sacrifice of our Passover Lamb, Yeshua the Messiah.

Family
Next year in the New Jerusalem!

Leader
The prescribed order of the Passover service is now complete. May we remember throughout the year that our redemption is complete by the sacrifice of our Passover Lamb, Yeshua the Messiah.

Family
Next year in the New Jerusalem!

FAMILY
CELEBRATIONS
AT
EASTER

INSTRUCTIONS:
EASTER TREE

Materials

* One tree branch (lightweight, but with lots of small branches)
* One pot or vase for holding tree branch
* Soil or rocks for weighting down pot or vase
* One piece of pastel colored posterboard
* Crayons or washable markers
* Scissors
* Glue or gluestick
* Paperpunch
* Yarn, string, or metal ornament hooks

Instructions for Making Holiday Tree

1. Set tree branch in pot or vase. Support the tree branch by filling the vase or pot with soil or rocks. This will be the holiday tree itself.

2. Photocopy the symbols for the holiday tree on pp. 156–177 of this book.

3. The entire family can color the symbols, using crayons, markers, paints—whatever medium you chose.

4. Cut out the circles. Even small children can help as long as they have blunt-end scissors.

5. Using one of the circles as a pattern, draw 24 circles on the piece of posterboard. Adults or older children will have to cut out these circles.

6. Glue the paper circles with the colored symbols onto the poster board circle backings. This is fun and easy for the small ones to do, especially if they have gluesticks.

7. On the posterboard backing, write the day and the Scripture verse which correspond to each symbol.

8. Optional: at this point, you may want to bring your circles to a print shop and have them laminated. This is an inexpensive way to ensure that the circles will last for years to come.

9. Punch a hole in the top of each circle, about 1/4 inch from the edge.

10. Cut 24 lengths of yarn or string. Each length should be about 10 to 12 inches. (Optional: simply use ornament hooks which you can buy inexpensively at the drugstore. Yarn is safer to use with small children, however.)

11. Tie strings through holes in circles.

To Use the Holiday Tree

1. Keep the circles (symbols) in a manila envelope or a plastic bag.

2. Before each devotional time, find the symbol which is indicated for that day's reading.

3. At the conclusion of the family devotions, allow a child to place the symbol on the tree. You may have to hang several symbols on each branch.

SYMBOL PATTERNS

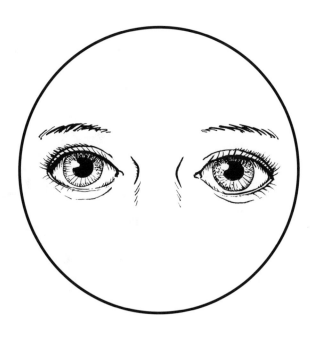

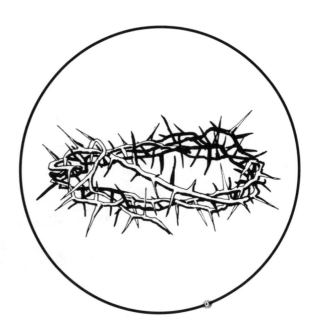

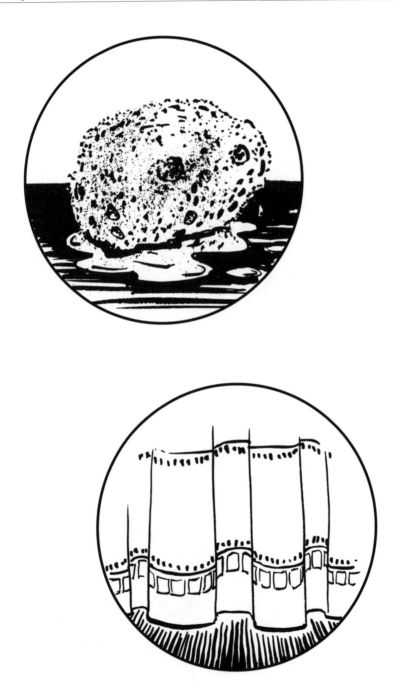

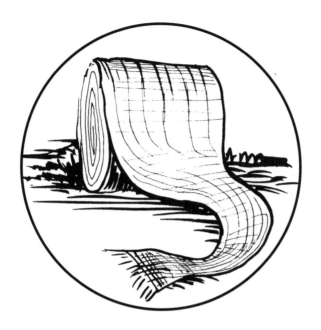

FAMILY
CELEBRATIONS
AT
EASTER

HYMNS

I Lay My Sins on Jesus

1 I lay my sins on Je - sus, The spot - less Lamb of God;
2 I lay my wants on Je - sus; All full - ness dwells in him;
3 I rest my soul on Je - sus, This wea - ry soul of mine;

He bears them all and frees us From the ac - curs - ed load.
He heals all my dis - eas - es; My soul he does re - deem.
His right hand me em - brac - es; I on his breast re - cline.

I bring my guilt to Je - sus To wash my crim - son stains
I lay my griefs on Je - sus, My bur - dens and my cares;
I love the name of Je - sus, Im - man - uel, Christ, the Lord;

Clean in his blood most pre - cious Till not a spot re - mains.
He from them all re - leas - es; He all my sor - rows shares.
Like fra - grance on the breez - es His name a - broad is poured.

Crown Him with Many Crowns

1 Crown him with man - y crowns, The Lamb up - on his throne; Hark,
2 Crown him the vir - gin's Son, The God in - car - nate born, Whose
3 Crown him the Lord of love— Be - hold his hands and side, Rich
4 Crown him the Lord of life, Who tri - umphed o'er the grave And

how the heav'n - ly an - them drowns All mu - sic but its own. A -
arm those crim - son tro - phies won Which now his brow a - dorn; Fruit
wounds, yet vis - i - ble a - bove, In beau - ty glo - ri - fied. No
rose vic - to - rious in the strife For those he came to save. His

wake, my soul, and sing Of him who died for thee, And
of the mys - tic rose, Yet of that rose the stem, The
an - gels in the sky Can ful - ly bear that sight, But
glo - ries now we sing, Who died and rose on high, Who

hail him as thy match - less king Through all e - ter - ni - ty.
root whence mer - cy ev - er flows, The babe of Beth - le - hem.
down - ward bend their burn - ing eyes At mys - ter - ies so bright.
died, e - ter - nal life to bring, And lives that death may die.

Christ the Lord Is Risen Today; Alleluia!

1 Christ the Lord is ris'n to-day; Al - le - lu - ia!
2 For the sheep the Lamb has bled, Al - le - lu - ia!
3 Hail, the vic - tim un - de - filed, Al - le - lu - ia!
4 Chris-tians, on this ho - ly day, Al - le - lu - ia!

Chris-tians, has-ten on your way; Al - le - lu - ia!
Sin - less in the sin - ner's stead. Al - le - lu - ia!
God and sin-ners rec - on - ciled, Al - le - lu - ia!
All your grate-ful hom - age pay; Al - le - lu - ia!

Of - fer praise with love re - plete, Al - le - lu - ia!
Christ the Lord is ris'n on high; Al - le - lu - ia!
When con-tend - ing death and life, Al - le - lu - ia!
Christ the Lord is ris'n on high; Al - le - lu - ia!

At the pas - chal vic - tim's feet. Al - le - lu - ia!
Now he lives, no more to die. Al - le - lu - ia!
Met in strange and awe - some strife. Al - le - lu - ia!
Now he lives, no more to die. Al - le - lu - ia!

My Song Is Love Unknown

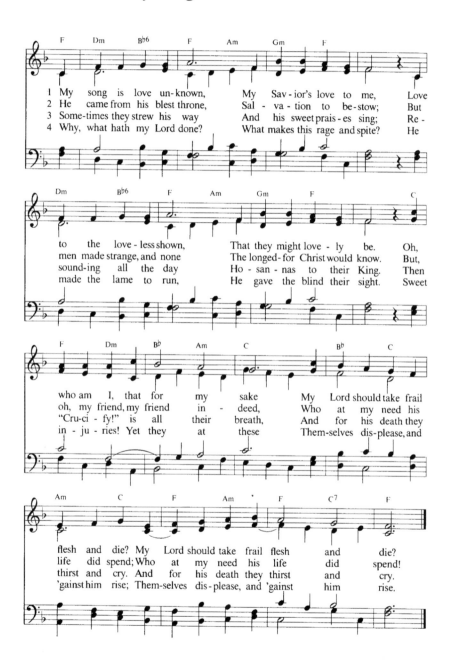

O Sacred Head, Now Wounded

1 O sa-cred head, now wound-ed, With grief and shame weighed down,
2 How art thou pale with an-guish, With sore a-buse and scorn;
3 What lan-guage shall I bor-row To thank thee, dear-est friend,
4 Lord, be my con-so-la-tion; Shield me when I must die;

Now scorn-ful-ly sur-round-ed With thorns, thine on-ly crown;
How does that vis-age lan-guish Which once was bright as morn!
For this thy dy-ing sor-row, Thy pit-y with-out end?
Re-mind me of thy Pas-sion When my last hour draws nigh.

O sa-cred head, what glo-ry, What bliss till now was thine!
Thy grief and bit-ter Pas-sion Were all for sin-ners' gain;
Oh, make me thine for-ev-er, And, should I faint-ing be,
These eyes, new faith re-ceiv-ing, From thee shall nev-er move;

Yet, though de-spised and gor-y, I joy to call thee mine.
Mine, mine was the trans-gres-sion, But thine the dead-ly pain.
Lord, let me nev-er, nev-er Out-live my love to thee.
For he who dies be-liev-ing Dies safe-ly in thy love.

When I Survey the Wondrous Cross

All Glory, Laud, and Honor

Refrain

All glo - ry, laud, and hon - or To you, re - deem - er, king,

To whom the lips of chil - dren Made sweet ho - san - nas ring.

1. You are the king of Is - rael And Da - vid's roy - al Son,
2. The com - pa - ny of an - gels Are prais - ing you on high;
3. The mul - ti - tude of pil - grims With palms be - fore you went.
4. To you, be - fore your Pas - sion, They sang their hymns of praise.

Refrain

Now in the Lord's name com - ing, Our King and Bless - ed One.
Cre - a - tion and all mor - tals In cho - rus make re - ply.
Our praise and prayer and an - thems Be - fore you we pre - sent.
To you, now high ex - alt - ed, Our mel - o - dy we raise.

The King of Love My Shepherd Is

1 The King of love my shep-herd is, Whose good - ness
2 Where streams of liv - ing wa - ter flow, My ran - somed
3 Per - verse and fool - ish oft I strayed, But yet in
4 In death's dark vale I fear no ill, With thee, dear

fail - eth nev - er; I noth - ing lack if
soul he lead - eth And, where the ver - dant
love he sought me, And on his shoul - der
Lord, be - side me, Thy rod and staff my

I am his And he is mine for - ev - er.
pas - tures grow, With food ce - les - tial feed - eth.
gent - ly laid, And home, re - joic - ing, brought me.
com - fort still; Thy cross be - fore to guide me.

5 Thou spreadst a table in my sight;
  Thine unction grace bestoweth;
And, oh, what transport of delight
  From thy pure chalice floweth!

6 And so, through all the length of days,
  Thy goodness faileth never.
Good Shepherd, may I sing thy praise
  Within thy house forever.

My Faith Looks Up to Thee

1 My faith looks up to thee, Thou Lamb of Cal - va - ry,
2 May thy rich grace im - part Strength to my faint - ing heart,
3 While life's dark maze I tread And griefs a - round me spread,
4 When ends life's tran - sient dream, When death's cold, sul - len stream

Sav - ior di - vine! Now hear me while I pray, Take all my
My zeal in - spire; As thou hast died for me, Oh, may my
Be thou my guide; Bid dark - ness turn to day, Wipe sor - row's
Shall o'er me roll; Blest Sav - ior, then, in love Fear and dis -

guilt a - way, Oh, let me from this day Be whol - ly thine!
love to thee Pure, warm, and change - less be, A liv - ing fire!
tears a - way, Nor let me ev - er stray From thee a - side.
trust re - move; Oh, bear me safe a - bove, A ran - somed soul!

Jesus Christ Is Risen Today

1 Je - sus Christ is ris'n to - day, Al - le - lu - ia!
2 Hymns of praise then let us sing, Al - le - lu - ia!
3 But the pains which he en - dured, Al - le - lu - ia!
4 Sing we to our God a - bove, Al - le - lu - ia!

Our tri - um-phant ho - ly day, Al - le - lu - ia!
Un - to Christ, our heav'n - ly king, Al - le - lu - ia!
Our sal - va - tion have pro - cured; Al - le - lu - ia!
Praise e - ter - nal as his love; Al - le - lu - ia!

Who did once up - on the cross, Al - le - lu - ia!
Who en-dured the cross and grave, Al - le - lu - ia!
Now a - bove the sky he's king, Al - le - lu - ia!
Praise him, all you heav'n-ly host, Al - le - lu - ia!

Suf - fer to re-deem our loss. Al - le - lu - ia!
Sin - ners to re-deem and save. Al - le - lu - ia!
Where the an - gels ev - er sing. Al - le - lu - ia!
Fa - ther, Son, and Ho - ly Ghost. Al - le - lu - ia!

Jesus, the Very Thought of You

1 Je - sus, the ver - y thought of you Fills us with sweet de - light;
2 No voice can sing, no heart can frame, Nor can the mind re - call
3 O Hope of ev - 'ry con - trite soul, O Joy of all the meek,
4 O Je - sus, be our joy to - day; Help us to prize your love;

But sweet-er far your face to view And rest with - in your light.
A sweet-er sound than your blest name, O Sav - ior of us all!
How kind you are to those who fall! How good to those who seek!
Grant us at last to hear you say: "Come, share my home a - bove."

Beneath the Cross of Jesus

1 Be-neath the cross of Je - sus I long to take my stand;
2 Up - on the cross of Je - sus, My eye at times can see
3 I take, O cross, your shad - ow For my a - bid - ing place;

The shad - ow of a might - y rock With - in a wea - ry land,
The ver - y dy - ing form of one Who suf - fered there for me.
I ask no oth - er sun - shine than The sun - shine of his face;

A home with-in a wil - der - ness, A rest up - on the way,
And from my con - trite heart, with tears, Two won - ders I con - fess:
Con - tent to let the world go by, To know no gain nor loss,

From the burn - ing of the noon - tide heat And bur - dens of the day.
The won - der of his glo - rious love And my un - wor - thi - ness.
My sin - ful self my on - ly shame, My glo - ry all, the cross.

191

Jesus, Priceless Treasure

1 Je - sus, price-less trea - sure, Source of pur - est plea - sure, Tru - est
2 In thine arm I rest me; Foes who would mo - lest me Can - not
3 Hence, all fears and sad - ness, For the Lord of glad - ness, Je - sus,

friend to me: Ah, how long I've pant - ed, And my heart has
reach me here. Though the earth be shak - ing, Ev - 'ry heart be
en - ters in. Those who love the Fa - ther, Though the storms may

faint - ed, Thirst-ing, Lord, for thee! Thine I am, O spot - less Lamb;
quak - ing, Je - sus calms my fear. Sin and hell in con - flict fell
gath - er, Still have peace with - in. Yea, what-e'er I here must bear,

I will suf - fer nought to hide thee, Nought I ask be - side thee.
With their bit - ter storms as - sail me, Je - sus will not fail me.
Still in thee lies pur - est plea-sure, Je - sus, price-less trea - sure!

If You But Trust in God to Guide You

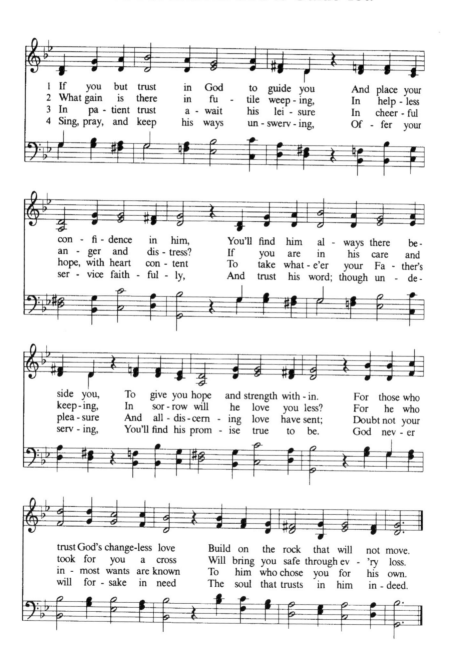

1 If you but trust in God to guide you
  And place your con - fi - dence in him,
  You'll find him al - ways there be - side you,
  To give you hope and strength with - in.
  For those who trust God's change-less love
  Build on the rock that will not move.

2 What gain is there in fu - tile weep - ing,
  In help - less an - ger and dis - tress?
  If you are in his care and keep - ing,
  In sor - row will he love you less?
  For he who took for you a cross
  Will bring you safe through ev - 'ry loss.

3 In pa - tient trust a - wait his lei - sure
  In cheer - ful hope, with heart con - tent
  To take what - e'er your Fa - ther's plea - sure
  And all - dis - cern - ing love have sent;
  Doubt not your in - most wants are known
  To him who chose you for his own.

4 Sing, pray, and keep his ways un - swerv - ing,
  Of - fer your ser - vice faith - ful - ly,
  And trust his word; though un - de - serv - ing,
  You'll find his prom - ise true to be.
  God nev - er will for - sake in need
  The soul that trusts in him in - deed.

Just as I Am, without One Plea

1 Just as I am, with-out one plea, But that thy blood was shed for me,
2 Just as I am, and wait-ing not To rid my soul of one dark blot,
3 Just as I am, though tossed a-bout With man-y a con-flict, man-y a doubt,
4 Just as I am, poor, wretch-ed, blind; Sight, rich-es, heal-ing of the mind,

And that thou bidd'st me come to thee,
To thee, whose blood can cleanse each spot,
Fight-ings and fears with-in, with-out,
Yea, all I need, in thee to find,

O Lamb of God, I come, I come.

5 Just as I am, thou wilt receive,
Wilt welcome, pardon, cleanse, relieve;
Because thy promise I believe,
O Lamb of God, I come, I come.

6 Just as I am; thy love unknown
Has broken ev'ry barrier down;
Now to be thine, yea, thine alone,
O Lamb of God, I come, I come.

Alas! And Did My Savior Bleed

1 A - las! And did my Sav - ior bleed, And did my sov - 'reign die?
2 Was it for sins that I had done He groaned up - on the tree?
3 Well might the sun in dark - ness hide And shut its glo - ries in
4 Thus might I hide my blush - ing face While his dear cross ap - pears,

Would he de - vote that sa - cred head For sin - ners such as I?
A - maz - ing pit - y, grace un-known, And love be - yond de - gree!
When God, the might - y mak - er, died For his own crea - tures' sin.
Dis - solve my heart in thank - ful - ness, And melt my eyes to tears.

5 But tears of grief cannot repay
   The debt of love I owe;
   Here, Lord, I give myself away:
   It's all that I can do.

Rock of Ages, Cleft for Me

1 Rock of A - ges, cleft for me, Let me hide my - self in thee;
2 Not the la - bors of my hands Can ful - fill thy law's de - mands;
3 Noth-ing in my hand I bring; Sim - ply to thy cross I cling.
4 While I draw this fleet - ing breath, When mine eye - lids close in death,

Let the wa - ter and the blood, From thy riv - en side which flowed,
Could my zeal no res - pite know, Could my tears for - ev - er flow,
Na - ked, come to thee for dress; Help - less, look to thee for grace;
When I soar to worlds un-known, See thee on thy judg-ment throne,

Be of sin the dou - ble cure: Cleanse me from its guilt and pow'r.
All for sin could not a - tone; Thou must save, and thou a - lone.
Foul, I to the foun - tain fly; Wash me, Sav - ior, or I die.
Rock of A - ges, cleft for me, Let me hide my - self in thee.

Index of Hymns